MY TALK - BOOK ELEVEN

In all I see, I see beauty within
I see the waterfall of life
Deadline
Timeline

In all I see, I see different worlds
I see instability
Fighting
War
Different faces
Races

I see hatred
Prejudice
Racism
Religious divide and confusion

In all I see, I know the truth
The truth of life and death

Michelle Jean

As the dreams come and go, I truly have to ask you Lovey, **WHAT ABOUT DECEMBER?**

What does December mean to you, and are you true to this month; December?

What does good and true life mean to you? Because in all I know and see, *I see my own anger, see the hatred and severe hostility towards the black race. I see and know my own anger when it comes to the treatment of my own black race based on hue.* (Babylonians excluded)

In all I see and know, I see and know the class divide; the one percent versus the millionaires, verses the upper middle class and the severely poor and destitute of this earth.

I see and know the cultural divide.
I see and know the religious divide and hatred; confusion and sacrifices that humans make; do.

In all I see and know, I see and know the God lie.
I see war on earth and war in the heavens; universe. I see war coming to earth.
Know the extinction of man.

But in all that I see and know, what about us; your good and true people Lovey and Good God?

Who is going to save us because you did not tell me I was the saving grace for our good and true people.

You told me to write a book and you did give me seeds to plant over 100 million acres. I told you, I need good seeds, good seeds that grow and have more good seeds. I truly do not want or need bad seeds Lovey. You are the MOTHER AND FATHER OF MY CHOICE and in all my choosing, I choose cleanliness and goodness; truth and righteousness for our people for more than infinite and indefinite lifetimes and generations more than forever ever. This means our people cannot walk in the way of sin; wickedness and evil for more than forever ever without end, and more than infinitely and indefinitely. We must not know sin and wickedness; evil. Hence we cannot under any circumstances live amongst and with wicked and evil; sinful, vile and unclean including spirits and animal. This also includes wicked and evil; sinful and unclean environments and waters. **_Everything that we do must be totally void of all sin and evil._** All that we do must be absolutely clean, good, positive and true; pure all around. You know this is my desire Lovey. Hence I make absolutely no provision for anyone or anything including animals and environment that is wicked and evil, unclean and sinful; dirty. Our environment including sex and procreating must be good, clean and true; positive and honest; pure at all times. Total truth must we have hence lies we cannot tell; must not tell. We must speak the truth at all times. There are no costs to truth Lovey, but there is a cost associated with lies, and that cost is death and you Lovey know this. Hence you cannot continue to let us; our good and true people including me live amongst the defiled and unclean; wicked and evil of this world and universe come on now.

You know for a fact that when we live amongst liars, we become liars also.

If we live in sin, we will become sinful and we are sinful Lovey. Look at the state of humanity today.

Look at the state of humanity in the past. Nations colonizing nations and robbing them of You, their language, heritage, good clothing, good life and sex life, good food and spiritual well being. These nations brought war and death to a once peaceful and clean nation. Hence good can never live with evil because evil, control, dominate and destroy; kill. Can a good man woman or child truly praise you in unclean land and lands? Will their praise not be condemned; be defiled because they are praising you in an unclean environment? You know the truth Lovey but have done nothing truthfully to rectify the problem. ***So as our praise go up to you unclean, are we not unclean*** *also? **WILL OUR BLESSING (S) NOT COME DOWN AND OR BACK TO US UNCLEAN ALSO? NO ONE CAN CO-EXIST WITH EVIL NO MATTER THE CIRCUMSTANCE (S)** come on **now.*** Not even you can live with or amongst evil; unclean people and spirits including animals. You do all to separate yourself from unclean lands and people, so why let your people continue to co-habitate and with the defiled; unclean? So come December, December 2015 all that wicked and evil nations and people do, must come to an end. If not abruptly Lovey then gradually forever ever without end. You must not give rise to the superiority of race ever again because **WHITE; THE WHITE RACE IS NOT GREATER THAN LIFE; THEY ARE DEATH; SPIRITUAL AND PHYSICAL DEATH.**

They come with death and give death; hence the many diseases that they come with throughout the ages to wipe out other races including their own. Those whites who do not fall under the banner of Death; white, but those who fall under the banner of Life; Black. So there are no superiority of race because **whites picky back off blacks; black people** and you and I know this because you've shown me this. ***They (the white and black race) have forgotten that they are from the same bloodline and descent.*** Hence the war between good and evil has and have continued over the ages; centuries. This war and hatred must stop more than infinitely and indefinitely forever ever without end as of now; December 2015. Family cannot continue to fight family because as it is; ***DEATH IS WINNING AGAINST MAN.*** Hence the enmity must stop Lovey. *You did not put enmity there; evil did. Look at it, are you not keeping good and evil alive despite the atrocities evil has done to the different nations of this globe.*

Evil matters not your race; skin colour; agenda. All that matters to evil is sustaining the life of death, and the perfect way to do this is to get everyone to sin; go against you Lovey and evil is doing that. As it is right now, ***billions are slated to die and are going to die in hell.*** Humanity knows not the confines of hell and I've tried my best to show humanity this in many of these books.

AS HUMANS WE MAKE LIFE CHOICES.

Meaning the life we live in the living (physical) determines where you go in the afterlife and or once the spirit leaves the flesh. So if you have more sin on your death record and less sin on your life record, then you are going to go to hell and burn.

Your spirit is going to become extinct because sin and or death was your life choice in the living. If you have more good on your good record and less sin on your death record, then you are going up to life; yes you are going to see Lovey; Good God and Allelujah.

What if
But

Confusion is setting in I know. For billions of you, death is your reality. Lovey gave me seeds and I know what those seeds are. **_They are these books and not humans._ _But because I've chosen to let my readers be my good books; chosen; then the good that I do, goes towards saving them also._** So at the end of my journey, if I have more than infinite and infinite number of good on my Life Record, those good go towards Lovey, who is my true and unconditional and immeasurable love, my more than beautiful and gorgeous mother Rosalind Rosetta Morgan, my great grandmother and somewhat my grandmother, my children, sister and brothers and you my true and dedicated readers. As for my immediate family, sister and brothers this can so change but for now no. And no I will not exclude the earth because these more than infinite and infinite number of good also go towards the beautiful and gorgeous trees of life, my beautiful waterways, rivers and oceans, seas, streams, the universe and earth herself and the land and lands of my choosing; well bask about anyway. These lands are Kenya, China, Russia, and deep down my homeland Jamaica but not the wicked and evil people of Jamaica. Yes Cayman you are there because Lovey did choose you (the Cayman Islands) for his home to be built in. And for all you skeptic, I will have a condo in Russia come hell or high water and please don't ask me why. Yes they have pretty skin, hence the deliciousness of them also. In a way for some strange reason, I want and need Lovey to maintain the oil sands in this land (Russia) and Canada but take the oil sands from Saudi Arabia, Iraq, Iran, and Nigeria, and to a large extent South Sudan. Well at least put South Sudan on hold because life did join in this land, and I have a soft spot for this country. Skin tone people. Very black and gorgeous. Tall and humble people and I truly like them. Wow. They are like cute and delicious because when I see the darkness of these people, I can think of the foundation of life and how beautiful and gorgeous that foundation (the foundation of life) is.

Onwards I go because I've gotten too over board.

And for all of you that say I am racist and why want the oil sands to be taken from Saudi Arabia. The spiritual world and or realm including me, truly don't like them. So for the spiritual realm I have no issues or problems with you in regards to taking away the oil sands from Saudi Arabia because you want to do it anyway. So if I am your petition and or permission to take this substance (black gold, crude oil; the oil sands) from Saudi Arabia, you have my good and true blessings to do so without bad blood and regret. You have my more than indefinite and more than forever ever approval to take the oil sands from Saudi Arabia. Wicked and evil are they hence your will shall be done and permission granted because you've been itching to do this from long ago it seems.

LOVEY, YOU ARE THE MOTHER AND FATHER THAT I CHOSE FOR OUR GOOD AND TRUE PEOPLE.

***YOU ARE THE MOTHER AND FATHER THAT I CHOSE FOR MY EARTHLY AND SPIRITUAL CHILDREN; ALL THAT YOU'VE GIVEN ME IN GOODNESS AND IN TRUTH.** So truly do not disappoint us including me.*

Truly do not leave us basking in sin; our sins, and the sins of others that are around us anymore. Truly protect and guide us in all that you do. You are our trust and hope and right now I am losing hope. *I am at the stage yet again where I want to go home and disappoint and or abandon you, but you will not let me. You keep protecting you. I've told family yet again that I am going home if my life do not pick up for the positive; better good come September of this year. And you've told me yet again, if I go home I will be imprisoned; die of medical need. But with all this said, isn't the spiritual realm hypocritical and dishonest when it comes to truth Lovey? No Lovey, see with me because I am confused. He, this white man told me Jamaica and Japan is going to be destroyed, but yet here you are telling me that I will be imprisoned for 25 years in Jamaica, and I will die in prison of medical need.* <u>**Yes the imprisonment is because of the stance I take with the Jamaica nasty and sellout government.**</u> *Di obeah working rectobate dem wey inna office inna Jamaica wey a kill di people dem slowly and dem di fool fool Jamaican people cannot see this. Yes I was offered the job of Prime Minister in Jamaica by him in the spiritual realm twice and I turned him down because of truth Lovey. You did not tell me to run for Prime Minister, you told me to write a book. So if HE DI WHITE MAN SEY JAMAICA AND JAPAN A GOH BI DESTROYED, HOW AM I GOING TO BE IMPRISONED? Yes I know he did not tell me when Jamaica and Japan is going to be destroyed, but Lovey, why confuse me? Nuff tings, yu noa wha mek mi figet it because I know white people dreams are false to a large degree. They* *have no truth or merit to them when it comes to me. White people lie, hence I take them (white spirits) with a grain of salt in the spiritual realm. Dem too damn deceiving. So as they are deceiving in the spiritual realm, they are deceiving in the physical realm. Yes not all, hence I am not generalizing when it comes to the white race based on HUE AND HUE ALONE; NOT DEEDS.*

In all I've asked, I've asked for forever ever goodness and truth; cleanliness, true and good prosperity that grow up to you not down for our people Lovey.

They (our good and true people) cannot stray from you and go on the other side anymore. One bad apple cannot spoil the whole bunch because I am expecting you, to take away all that is wicked and evil; sinful from our genes; DNA, our land and lands and surroundings including waters and seas; trees, the environment. I truly do not need part time people that's going to say they love you but behind your back, they stab you in it, sell you out and abandon you; do all that is wicked and evil to kill you. Like I've told you, my greatest fear is losing you, but you can no longer let your people which is our people continue to live in pain and hardship; suffering. You cannot continue to let us live with and amongst death's people. Evil destroy and kill and you fail to realize this.

Evil take away from all Lovey and you truly know this; fail to comprehend this. **You cannot pree and or want cleanliness and leave us in unclean lands; places. We are not clean when you do this, we are dirty.**

Lovey, you see my struggles with my children and how they do not listen. I am battling to stay alive right now and it's not an easy feat. I have to be mother and father and no matter how I put you at the elm; head; problems still come my way via children and family and occasionally others. As a parent you want and need what's best for your children but they do not want and need what's best for self. It's as if the ambition is not there. They do not see the sacrifice you are making for them. I stand alone because in many ways, I am alone and you've left me on my own. Yes I complain to you constantly and I can't anymore, I have to move on.

No one can stay in pain for too long. At some point or another something have to give and something did give, hence billions have and has walked away from you and you cannot blame them. *So in all that you do for me and more, as of December, December 2015, let our children including my children and black people based on hue and deeds, good deeds begin to listen to your good and true counsel Lovey. We have to start listening to you in order for us to save ourselves come on now.*

Yes I see and know that you've tried, but what about the ones that truly want to come home. Yes I am being called home but where I am being called home to, I truly do not know.

Remember, men lie in the spiritual realm hence many a times I am left trying to decipher and or trying to figure out what's been told to me. Yes the spiritual realm can be deceptive; hence I know the deception of men in both worlds; the physical and spiritual. As our guideline Lovey, you leave us to ward off evil and sometimes we cannot. We need you, but you've shown us that you don't need us.

If we are your good and true light, why not be our good and true light also?

If we are your good and true light, then truly light our way so that we cannot fail you or fall from you or your grace ever again.

If we are your light, then be our true way come on now. You and I both know that we cannot live without you. So what's wrong? Am I not trying to change all the wrongs in my life?

I've told you, I want to move out and leave my children. One I will carry because he listens to good and true counsel. Hence I will forever ever without end make a good way for him in the living and in the spirit. My other children I cannot deal with them because they want to learn things the hard way. They do wrongs and no matter how I talk to them, they do not listen. Yes my second one changed in some ways but in truth he's all talk. I need to move from him especially. No, I truly need to move from all of them, but I have to make a good way for my first child. You know this Lovey. I am trying to do your work but some of my children are shattering it and will shatter it due to deeds; what they do. I know we are not all clean, just look at my slate before I was called. I did have blemishes on my record; hence I am hoping my slate is totally clean right now. **_Respect is due Lovey, but you cannot live amongst and or with people that do not respect you. Nor can you live amongst and or with people that do not have the same values as you._**

I cannot under any circumstances live with and or amongst people that do not have good and clean values. I am trying to make my way more than perfect and clean with you. I need to have a pure and more than clean heart, and yes I need to be slow to anger. Hence I cannot live in the society and societies of men; humans. **_I need to truly live in your clean society where morals are valued._**

You keep me in a lawless society and it does hurt me, hence many times I tell you I am *leaving. And despite you telling me and showing me my death, <u>I want to walk into the fire. Not because of disobedience or lack of respect, but because I cannot take anymore hell in my life.</u> I need true happiness, and you cannot give me this nor can you make me truly happy.*

I need a pure and clean environment where I can talk to you face to face and you cannot give me this.

It's June 24, 2015 and this morning I kept dreaming about Carnival and Jouvert People and or Music which is Carnival. Lovey I was shown the ugliness of Jouvert and or Carnival and I don't want or need to be associated with this (carnivals).

CARNIVALS ARE A SIN.

Lovey, this was shown to me on this day, June 24, 2015. I knew jouvert was duppy ting for which I call duppy art. Carnivals praise the dead.

Carnivals are sinful because when carnival time comes, you get on bad; parade for the dead. Hence giving the dead praise and worship. **<u>You are not celebrating life, you are celebrating the dead; the demons of hell.</u>** Hence voodoo and obeah rituals cannot stop. You are giving your soul over to death; the daemons of hell to possess you and kill you; take you directly to hell. Carnivals are like graven images of death. ***You as carnival goers are making and or painting yourself up as the dead; thus you are the graven image and images of death.*** You dance around the idols of death because you idolize death. This is no different from the story of Moses and when he came down from the mount and saw his people parading and dancing around a Hindu God, the golden calf. Thus black people know not of their roots and how Egypt was conquered and subjected to false gods and worship, language and religion. ***Every good and true Black Civilization were conquered and assimilated into the devils own; society.*** We, our black ancestors were beaten and tortured to accept death. No not all but our own blacks did help Death and or Satan and or the Devil to conquer their own. Nimrod was a prime example of this. Hence **BLACK PEOPLE CAN BE FOUND IN INDIA UNTIL THIS DAY.** Yes blacks were in Pakistan too; hence statues still stand erect in honour or our Black ancestors until this day. Yes I was told this by a Pakistani. I've never been to Pakistan myself to validate this and have no plans to either. **Hence BLACK CULTURE HAVE AND HAS BE RAPED AND DISTORTED BY ALL GLOBALLY.**

Carnivals give the demons of hell an all access pass to you and your soul but many people do not know this. Now look at it Lovey, who is keeping up with the trend? Look at the black nations globally especially in the Caribbean, North and South America. So now tell me, if we as black people truly loved you and belonged to you, would we be celebrating death like this and disrespecting you?

Yes people enjoy themselves, but do we need to masquerade around looking like the dead; demons of hell?

Why the costumes and body paint?

If we want to celebrate Lovey, why not celebrate life? Eat and drink, dance and listen to your good up good up music and let this celebration be about goodness, good and true life come on now.

We say we have life but yet do not celebrate life, we celebrate death. So when death comes, no one should complain come on now.

Have mercy Lovey because after seeing this man and how ugly he is, I truly have to turn to you. I have to celebrate life in the park with some good music that lifts up my soul and spirit; You. I cannot parade around looking like a fool wearing next to nothing because this is truly not what you are all about. Yes, I like nudity, but in my home and not on the streets. I know she wanted me to end up naked and in the streets. She did try, but she failed. Lovey many things was done to me but I am still standing. Therefore I have to leave wicked and evil people and lands to time because I know their end in time. ***DEATH IS TIME, BUT LIFE HATH NO TIME LIMIT. TIME IS FOREVER EVER WITHOUT END.*** All that is and or are wicked and evil hath time, but the one thing that humans do not know nor do they comprehend, is the time in time when they must die. ***The magnitude of time they cannot over stand, hence women are the keepers of time. They tell time and will always tell time due to the womb; cycle of time; her period which is the shedding of her blood; her menstrual cycle. Hence humans know not the power and strength; truth of female death.*** So yes for all you carnival goers that think you have a say, you have none because all of you have sinned and that sin is on your sin record.

Yes there is more that I saw because I am interrupting the flow of this book. But this is me in these books; always interrupting the flow.

And if anyone of you wanted to know after seeing this (carnival truth) I saw this black man. You could see him changing from his state to this hideous state. Hence black people based on hue are changing from pretty to ugly. We are losing our beauty physically and spiritually. *(Babylonians excluded)*

And even though the majority of the Babylonian population have dark and or black skin, they are not included and or classed as black, they are classed as white. They do not have the same skin texture, nor do they have black people's hair, nor do they speak our true language. Nor are they of our heritage and lineage and more importantly descent.

Now this black man that was changing his state and projecting and or showing me his ugly state looked like Future Fambo; the I'm Drinking Rum and Redbull singer. <u>**The man in the dream was not him, but he had the same features and build without the tattoos.**</u> So you get an idea of what I am talking about. This is why I tell you, black people based on hue are changing from pretty to ugly.

I also dreamt me. I don't know if I was at a book fair, but it's a book something and my picture was in a book. It's like wow because my gray hair was gone. The picture looked good, yeah me. I was also enjoying myself at the book fair because I looked spunky. Man let's hope it's not the other way around. I truly need some happiness with these books.

I also dreamt I was in a conversation with someone about Jesus. I can't remember what happened, but I think I said, "can you find him?" but don't quote me on that. I am not sure if I told the person Jesus did not exist or if I asked, what colour was Jesus?

I know Revelations described him as being black and how he Jesus looked "LIKE THE SON OF MAN," and not the son of God. And yes Revelations specifically said, the son of man and not God just to add that in there.

In the dream it's like I had a newspaper and I could see Jesus, this white man, but when I tried showing the person who is black that I was talking to, I could not show the person the White Jesus that was in the newspaper. I could not find him and or his picture that was in the newspaper. Twice I tried but could not find this White Jesus.

I know I have to complete my book Blackman Redemption The Truth About Jesus real soon. I know what the dream means and what it is telling me. *I know we as black people was given A WHITE JESUS TO BELIEVE IN AND FOLLOW. A WHITE JESUS THAT DO NOT EXIST BECAUSE HE CANNOT BE FOUND AND WILL NEVER BE FOUND.*

AS BLACK PEOPLE WE'VE FORGOTTEN WHO OUR GOD IS.

WE'VE FORGOTTEN OUR SPIRITUAL CONNECTION WITH LOVEY. HENCE WE'VE LOST OUR PLACE WITH HIM.

Yes this is sad, sad that we distort and abuse our spiritual connection and when we get beat up, abused and misused we are running to him.

And please do not look at my situation because I've told you, **_she did this to me._** I do not know what I did to her for her to do what she did, but it's over now. **_I cannot nor will I forgive her for what she has done to me._** No people, I see my struggles, the struggles of many of you and I will never forgive her for the pain and suffering she has caused and inflicted in my life. What did I do to her for her to do this to me and my family?

Hence the person and or persons that commissioned her to do this to me, I forgive them not. Let condemnation turn on them for more than infinite and indefinite lifetimes and generations more than forever ever without end. I have no forgiveness in my heart for wicked and evil people because they knowingly and willingly set out to hurt others. I refuse to petition Lovey for any of them, nor will I have compassion for any of them.

Families like me were left hurting and in pain. We are suffering for what?

What did I do to err you so, that you had to tie me; want me to go naked in the streets and begging for bread like an insane woman?

My children suffered alongside me. They went without hence every worker of iniquity, every voodoo and obeah man and woman that tie people; do the works of iniquity, I condemn all of you globally in the name of Lovey, Good God and Allelujah forever ever without end. **_CURSED ARE THE LOTS OF YOU._** Hence wallow in your condemnation of curses with the demons and or daemons of hell more than infinitely and indefinitely for more than forever ever without end. Thus saith the Lord thy God meaning it is so. **_SO AS YOU CURSE AND TIE OTHERS, YOU_**

TOO ARE NOW CURSED AND TIED TO HELL AND DEATH, INCLUDING THE DEMONS OR DAEMONS OF HELL FOR MORE THAN INFINITE AND INDEFINITE LIFETIMES AND GENERATIONS MORE THAN FOREVER EVER WITHOUT END UNTIL YOUR EVENTUAL EXTINCTION; THE TIME COMES WHEN DEATH TRULY EXTINGUISH YOUR EVIL LIFE FORCE UNTIL YOU ARE NO MORE INDEFINITELY; CANNOT COME BACK TO LIFE EVER AGAIN DUE TO YOUR WICKED AND EVIL DEEDS; SINS. No resurrection have you because no dead can be resurrection. Good spirits must live hence your so called Jesus cannot and will never save you because ***HE TRULY DID NOT EXIST.*** Death exists hence your so called Jesus ***IS YOUR EXTINCTION; DEATH BECAUSE HE'S THE ONE YOU PRAISE AND WORSHIP; GIVE HOMEAGE TO.*** All that you have must be taken from you, and the hurt and pain you've caused on another human being and spirit must turn back on you infinitely and indefinitely without end. Lovey gave you all a talent, use your talent to do good not evil. No place Lovey must be found for soothsayers, shamans, obeah men and women, voodoo priests and priestesses. You are the head of us Lovey, hence we as your good and true people must unite with you in all that we do good and truthful.

As black people we can no longer buy into the White Jesus bullshit and or story. Yes Lovey, many people (black people) will condemn me but to be truly honest with you, I truly do not care. Just as how our ancestors condemned your messengers of old and now, they will condemn and reject me also. And like I've told you, I've done my job, that which you required of me and I am so truly good to go. ***SO IF THE BLACK RACE WANTS TO DIE ALL OVER AGAIN, SO BE IT BECAUSE HELL IS FULL OF BLACK PEOPLE AND RECRUITING MORE.** We gave you up Lovey, and now look at us. Begging for bread and without a home. Everyone choose death, choose death and look at the cost humans have to pay on earth and in the spiritual realm because of death!!*

SO WHY THE HELL SHOULD I CHOOSE DEATH IF I KNOW I AM NOT GOING TO LIFE BUT DIE? Yes I want to leave you but you keep cautioning me about my death.

LIFE GIVES LIFE; GOOD AND TRUE LIFE, BUT YET HERE ON EARTH, WE LIVE IN STRESS

AND PAIN; ORDEAL AND ALOT OF US DO CHOOSE DEATH JUST TO GET RID OF THE PAIN AND HURT. BUT UNFORTUNATELY, DEATH CANNOT SAVE ANYONE FROM THE NEXT LEVEL OF PAIN; WHICH IS FAR DEADLIER IN THE SPIRITUAL REALM THAN IT IS IN THE PHYSICAL REALM.

Yes the enemies of Good; You Lovey cause us to stray and flee you for death because of stress, and this is sad. It is truly sad that you cannot see our hurt and pain and truly help us in a good and true way.

I know you wanted your mega mansion but in truth I cannot provide one for you because I do not have the financial means to do so, and you are truly not working. I cannot tap into your financial resources because you are not allowing me to. So I have to let your mega mansion go. And in all honesty Lovey, Carnivals are not clean and I need a truly clean environment for you that do not have carnivals; jump ups that praise and worship the dead. The Cayman Islands have jump ups, so truly think and not contradict yourself with me. Yes I know the reason for your choice. This is due to virtually no violence in the Cayman Islands and a banking system that poise itself on truth; fairness from what I've read. Hence stability in the financial sector when it comes to the Cayman Islands. Yes I need what's best for you, so if we can find another Island apart from the Cayman Islands to build your true home please let me know. But you know what, no. Cayman is your choice and you know what's best.

I know Jamaica is not clean and the Jouvert Music (Carnival crap) must be cleaned up in the Cayman Islands in my book. They have to clean up self and in all honesty Lovey, why am I battling with you over the Cayman Islands so?

You want a house there, but because the land is not hilly I battle you. Yes the waterfalls and all that I truly need for you and me.

I don't know Lovey. Maybe I want to run down a hill and come crashing into you and you lift me up like a child and say that's my baby girl.

Maybe I want and need you to lift my feet off the ground when I am running to you.

Maybe I put you too much on a pedestal that I more than truly and unconditional over love you with all my truth.

I don't know, maybe I am crazy Lovey when it comes to you.

So what say you about December?

What about December when it comes to me and you?

I am listening to JUST TO BE CLOSE TO YOU by Fred Hammond. And Lovey; is this not what I want and need?

Is this not what your true people want and need?

So why can't we be close to you?

Why do you keep us waiting like this?

Do you not want and need to be close to us?

If we are your light Lovey, why stay so far from us?

Why let evil reach us?

Ah it's a different day now (June 25, 2015), and the death dreams are coming again. Well they've never left. I know death is coming for my family but who will die I truly do not know.

Man I am smelling evil; death but my children cannot smell it. Sometimes I smell this foul sulphuric odour that annoys me. Man stench is all around me. Yes I know for whom the sulphuric scent belongs but I am going to leave well enough alone. Ole people sey, who caane hear must feel and some a fi mi pickney dem a guh feel. Truss mi, when trouble knocking dung dem doorstep; wait no, Lovey let me move away from them into our good up good up home before trouble comes for them. Dem nuh listen an mi caane tek haade ease pickney nuh more.

Lovey wha wrong with mi tummuck?

Have mercy because I so have to have it checked out. My back was hurting me and it was as if I was on my stomach and it felt so sore from within. So now I have to ask you, what's wrong with my spirit? Is it getting sick because of these medications?

Lovey it's the first time I am feeling my stomach sore from within. So please let me know what to do to secure my stomach and spirit because this soreness is not normal. And no my stomach do not feel sore in the living; my waking hours. Yes sometimes it feels sore but that's due to the medication I am taking and the extreme sensitivity of my skin. But this feel, soreness in my sleeping state is truly weird.

Tell me is a death in my family going to make me ill and or hurt me to the core of my stomach?

No Lovey, I have to ask because sometimes I feel death, the death of someone. So what is going on that you are hiding from me?

I need to know the truth. This morning I dreamt I was going to a wedding and we were late. When we got to the wedding we were hours, I think three (3) hours late. The wedding did not start but we were late this I know. Weddings are usually death for me for some strange reason but this is changing. Someone I knew actually got married. I will not put anything into this wedding dream. I just have to wait and see what is going on in my personal family life. You know me, I am one away. The one that feels like the outcast and the disappointment of my family, hence I stay away from them. Yes I avoid my family like the plague because in many ways when I go around them and see their accomplishments, I feel like my children and me are a failures to them.

Am I jealous of what they have?

Hell no. It's just I feel like a failure around them. I feel like my children are a failure around them. Yes they have a better life than me, but that I worry not about because their accomplishments are their accomplishments. I am but one and they are but two. Yes I yearn for the day when I am free from these prison walls, but it does not make me feel any better. Yes I know what she did to me for me never to ever rise. But she's in hell now because I will never forgive her for what she did to me and yes she is condemned by you.

I'm still trying and one day I will make it. Let's just hope I am not in my seventies or eighties or sixties before I make it.

I will rise again; hence I am going through the struggles. I stay to myself and I truly like it this way. No one knows the struggles I go through except for you my readers and sometimes my sister and niece including brother and two other person.

Yes my children knows my struggles because they cause me pain. Hence I can't wait to get a place of my own and leave them the hell alone. So yes death comes now to my family this I truly know.

Can death be stopped?

Yes and you have the key. Living clean and true; positive and good is the key. And yes it's unfortunate that many cannot use this key to help themselves and others.

Also, dreamt this egg (balut). I saw the bird inside of it. The picture on Wikipedia is the same picture I saw in my dream. Yes this is a first for me.

Yes I dreamt about other things but I can't remember if the dream had to do with numbers. So I am going to leave things alone because at this point in my dream world, I truly don't know what to do with the black race on a whole.

I am missing something with them Lovey because I cannot comprehend why You KEEP OFFERING US GOOD AND TRUE LIFE AND BLACKS THE BLACK RACE (Babylonians excluded) KEEP REJECTING YOU FOR DEATH?

If you were to look at the black race based on hue (Babylonians excluded) we've become the people of Sodom and Gomorrah.

We embellish ourselves into things that are not ours. Hence we as black people (Babylonians excluded) do not know our true history and culture. Instead of sticking to our own, we accept things that are not our own and call it ours.

Lovey, we've lost our place with you because of these lies and we cannot see this. No wonder it's so hard for your messengers.

I cannot comprehend why we would believe in the lies of these wicked and evil people.

We've got the holy bible; your word many are saying. But I ask you and them Lovey, which word is holy?

Did you write the books of men?

Did you of yourself Lovey sit down and write these books, even publish them?

So how can man say the book of sin is holy?

Not even my books are holy. None can say they are despite the fact that you told me to write you a book, not once but twice.

So how can we as humans deem something holy when YOU OF YOURSELF DID NOT TELL US TO? You did not say, write my holy book because no human on the face of this planet know your original language and tongue. I've seen your language and I am sealed with this language, but I cannot write it, nor can I speak it. **No one can speak this language because it cannot be spoken only written.**

So Lovey what is life, true life without you and your goodness and truth?

Oh Lovey please don't leave me alone because I need you right now.

What is going on in my personal life with my family?

What is truly going on because I so want to change my phone number so that family cannot get to me. I am so getting fed up. Lovey this child knows nothing about my mother and shi a pitch pan har. Shi nuh noa sey mi crass when it comes to my mother. She is dead and gone, lef affa har now come on. Mi madda a badda har mek si a pitch pan har soh. Listen Lovey, I know I have to keep my cool and trust me it will be no problem to me not to speak to her. I will have absolutely no regret because mi nuh hitch up aunda family batty hole, soh mi nuh noa wey dis gyal a du. If mi cuss har, di wurl shame. So please help me to cool my temper because the devil dem inna fi mi family a get loose and dem nuh noa mi. Mi stubban and trust mi, I can walk away from my entire family with ease. I am one away; hence I am the outcast of my family. I put you Lovey above them and you know this. So please help me to truly contain my anger because duppy caane frighten mi. Demya BC duppy ya wey inna fi mi family nuh noa mi and mi anger. The temper is coming Lovey. A mi madda disya duppy a pitch pan and shi truly do not want me to burn har because I will devour her. Do not bleep roune mi madda because shi naah trouble yu. Lef har alone. I will tumble you down for her so step off man come on now.

Lovey, the devil naah stap with mi and mi tiad of the nonsense around me as well as in my life.

Lovey, you know what, let me put my anger in your hands because if I start hell will become cold literally. Truly help me to wane my anger Lovey because you know the fierceness of my anger. I maybe sick but the spirit is strong. Yes the body is weak, but I am strong in you spiritually. So please truly help me to curve my anger because fi mi cussing nuh good nor is it clean and you know this. **<u>No, I will not lift up arms against anyone. Hence these words are my strength and power in all that I do.</u>** Lovey, wow. Yu noa wha, let me focus on us and this song I am listening to. **MISS YOU SO MUCH by Dexta Daps and Blakkman.** Yes I miss my mother so much, hence I will defend her at all cost.

So Lovey truly thank you for her and tell her I truly miss her; wish she was here with me each and every day. She is my light and way also. So Lovey, in all that we do for each other, please remember her, and please let her be the first one you save for me. Yes Lovey I truly love her with all my truth and true love unconditionally just like you. You are both my praise and praises. Thank you to the both of you for being a part of my perfect world of truth and goodness; praise.

Lots of kisses Lovey because you did well by giving her (my mother) to me.

Ah Lovey, you know that I am a defender of you and her. Oh Lovey, I truly love MISS YOU SO MUCH, and although my mother is gone, she will never be forgotten because the both of you live on in me. You, both mothers, You and Mama, Miss Peggy (Rosalind Morgan) are my heartbeat and light, my perfection and perfect world. Thank you both for completing me.

Thank you both for always being there for me in all that you do. Never stop protecting me because you are both appreciated and you're all more than the greatest. Perfect are you both, hence our world is clean and pure; truly rich and more than mountainous in truth; true and more than unconditional love that is immeasurable.

Michelle

Lovey, if there is anything more I could do for you and her (my gorgeous and beautiful mother), I would do it in goodness and truth so long as your asking is good and clean.

Wow do I ever miss the both of you.

So because I miss the both of you so much, I dedicate this song (Miss You So Much) to the both of you. I know neither of you are dead because your spirit; energy lives on in me and the universe. But I do miss you guys.

And yes if I could see and speak to the both of you face to face each and every day I'd be okay. Wow, Lovey I miss you and Miss Peggy so much.

One day Lovey. Truly one day I will see you and Miss Peggy. One day we will be together truthfully.

One day we will sit and talk, laugh and enjoy each other. We will hold hands because my hands are outstretched to the both of you in thought right now. So as I journey towards the both of you, please take my hand and let's journey together as one and or in unison.

Michelle, June 25, 2015

Lovey smile for me.

Do you get angry like me?

Are you my great defender in all that I do?

Ah Lovey, never go away again from me.
Lovey, I know I wrote some things recently and I will include what I've written in this book because this book is entitled ***WHAT ABOUT DECEMBER?***

So Lovey, as your good and true people come home to you, hold on to us and never let us go ever again.

Never stay away from us because in truth, I truly do not want you to leave us or journey away from us ever again. The pain and suffering is not pretty.

Lovey we did lose our way and I do not need this lost way anymore. I need your true friendship to stay. I do miss you and you know this. **<u>Living without you is like a dried up river. We have no life; water to grow.</u>** Lovey you are truly needed never forget this.

Yes we've become broken and confused without you. I know I cannot live without you in my life but it's hard keeping track and or walking on your pathway. Too much stumbling blocks are in my way; hence I have to get rid of my physical family.

Dem too stressful and I cannot take the stress of them. Yes I am leaning on you and resting my head on your shoulder. So please truly comfort me because you are my comfort right now.

Ah Lovey, can we just go away. No not today but some other day. I am feeling better and it seems like someone is here in my apartment with me other than my children, and yes, she is a lady. So in all that you did and do, I truly thank you because I am feeling a lot better, and no I did not want to listen to Fred, I needed this song; ***MISS YOU SO MUCH.***

Oh Lovey, I may be weird but you are true. Hence I will always need you.

Like I said, one day we will be together and we will live in unison and peace. You are my true peace in my time and times of anger; need. So I leave my disturbers to you; leave them in your good and capable hands.

Michelle

Ah Lovey it's June 26, 2015 and I am asking you to let the storms be over in my life infinitely and indefinitely more than forever ever without end.

Lovey, you gave us (humans) a choice and many have and has chosen the latter and abandoned life. Yes I know why and looking at my situation and the situation of others, I truly cannot blame them (evil and my ancestors). Evil was let loose on earth and evil has not stopped devouring.

You're gone from us, hence we are left unprotected in hell; our physical hell and torture here on earth. You see this (our troubles and pain) and no matter how we cry to you for a saving grace for self, none comes. We are still here living amongst liars and thieves; murderers that rape us of our strength, pride and dignity; heritage and language, and more importantly YOU.

Yes I know you've asked me to write you a book twice, but was it worth it Lovey?

Was all this evil on earth worth it?

Look at your creation; good and true life and tell me, was the destruction worth it?

You gave death time, now look at the earth and the universe including the people of earth. So tell me, how can you ask us and or anyone to write if they are not true to you; us? I want to leave you due to hardship and pain and you can't blame me. Yes where I want to go you refuse to let me go, but instead of truly helping me, you leave me in a land that I want to escape from. **This land is my true spiritual prison and hell and you know this. But yet you keep me enslaved here. Now tell me, where is your fairness and truth to me?**

I want to leave you due to my ill health.
I want to leave you because I see the injustice of humans on this earth and it sickens me. It sickens me to see you stand aside and look; watch this wickedness and evil continue to go on.

Yes I've drawn a line between me and you, but you've crossed it, and I've crossed yours with my fury and anger at times. Now yesterday a family member caused me anger, and yes I came to you for comfort and I was comforted through song. I am better today, but the enemies that surround me must go; come out of my life because like I said, I can walk away from family without regret because I am the outsider; the outcast. I am not like them and I refuse to be like any of them. I am me and I've been through hell on this earth and I refuse to continue to go through hell with you or anyone. You don't break people man and I've been broken to the point of ill repair. All these things you do not see, but yet my spirit will not let me leave you nor will you let me leave you. *But Lovey, if evil continuously penetrate us and destroy us, what is the point of staying with you. DOES NOT EVIL DESTROY YOU ALSO? Are you not powerless against evil?*

Mother Earth is riddled with pain and suffering because she has to hide death in her. She has to keep the dry bones of man; humanity in her, and now I ask you this, is this truly fair to her?

Why should she keep the dry bones of evil; man?

Why should she continue to give the wicked and evil of this earth and universe a home?

Yes this morning I have questions, but in all of my questioning; truly what about December?

Lovey, as December comes shortly, can you and I have impenetrable frameworks and foundations between us? Meaning let no evil of any sort come between us. Let no evil separate and or divide us. Lovey, I need this for our good and true people also. I need impenetrable frameworks and foundations with you for them. No evil must conquer them and separate them from you no matter what. No evil must control and dominate them ever again including me and you. You; good and true life that grow up positively in goodness and in truth is what I need for them including me also. I also need a stress free and harmonious life that is filled with pure and true peace that fill the earth and their lives forever ever without end. No sacrifice must be made unto other gods Lovey. Absolutely none lest I be truly angry at you. You are the only true God that we are to know, keep and praise without end.

Lovey you are in me and you are my light and life force; so no evil should come near us. Lovey evil spirits should not come between us or near us come on now. So truly look into things because I truly don't want to lose you. I need true happiness always. So why can't you give this to me and our people? Why can't we work in unison to give them a happy home?

Lovey, we need to be more than solid, hence let evil go from this earth. Look at the death toll and destruction of this planet. Now another animal has and have become extinct due to the callousness of man; humans. Why?

Humans are the ones that are murderers. We kill for sport and we kill to eat. Why?

Look at the greedy and heartless that live upon this earth Lovey. Evil has no regard for life because they are greedy, wicked and evil. Thus evil societies are erected throughout the globe in honour of sin; the wickedness evil people do. Good life is not regarded when it comes to them, but yet they have the nerve to say one is going to die for them. Hence they sacrifice their own each and every day to their false gods without knowing that they themselves are condemned, and the more they kill, the longer they stay in hell and burn. Yes evil preserve death because humans are sins sacrifice unto his master death. Humans keep death alive with the sins they do each and every day. Hence billions have the last name of death and billions has his and her number thus the number 2 for many. Death in the physical and death in hell. So come December, December 2015, seal the faith of death by giving death what truly belongs to them. You cannot let earth continue to be a safe haven for the wicked and evil. You are unjust when you do this. I've told you what belongs to death belong to death. You cannot keep death's belongs. You are a liar and thief when you do this come on now. Hence rise me up in truth and true goodness Lovey, but never ever let me become greedy and heartless as the greedy and heartless of society; this world and universe. I need you to make me truly truthful and righteous in all that is good and true; positive and clean in you and me so that I can help this earth and universe, including our good and true people. Lovey impenetrable frameworks and foundations is what we need so that when the devil and their demons come to devour me and our good and true people, slander me and our good and true people; set us up, they more than stumble and fall. All that they do in evil towards me and our people must fall back on them more than infinitely and indefinitely without end. Evil can no longer devour good Lovey come on now. Evil must be stopped. You are good and true life, hence you are Allelujah. So good and true life must come back to earth and reign supreme forever more and forever ever without end.

Your good and true people are your good creation and you cannot continue to allow the devil to hinder us and kill us. This is not right. Do not ask us to do something for you and do not give us the proper tools to help you. We need the proper tools to till and maintain you and this land; earth. We need the proper tools to till and maintain you in the spiritual realm as well as in the universe. Give, but give properly; good and clean.

Help, but help cleanly and honestly.
Maintain, but maintain simply and organically; void of all evil; pesticides and herbicides.

Do not ask us to do something for you and keep us is sin. You are disrespecting our good and true right to a clean and pure; true and positive life; environment. You complain about us and yes you've given us rules, rules that billions break, but what about us, the ones that do not want or need to break your rules?

What about you?

Did you not leave us in environments that are inappropriate for us? Environments that make us disrespect you.

Environments that are unclean, filthy and dirty.

Have we not sinned reckless and rude here on earth? So tell me, how can you say you love us so, when you leave us in sin; alone?

A mother and father that truly loves their child cannot abandon them. I know this and I am learning this. And despite me wanting to leave my children, I cannot abandon them nor will I. You more than truly know this. No parent is that heartless. No, that's not true, some parents are that heartless and some do this. **<u>If you loved us so, would you not be doing all to take us out of sinful and evil; wicked and unclean environments?</u>**

I know you are keeping me out of Jamaica because you did deem the island unclean, and I thank you for that. But what about the one hundred and forty million plus that you have chosen for your true own? What about them Lovey?

What about us that truly want to be with you in a place that is void of all sin and evil; wickedness and pain; sorrow? What about us that want and need an environment that is totally clean and void of all unclean things including humans and animals, plants that maim and kill; stink?

Lovey, life is not death, but yet life is treated like death by society on a whole.

Remember you left us to live amongst the lawless and no matter how much I've prayed and bugged you for a better life and tomorrow; one that is void of all ills and pain; evil and sins; sorrow you've ignored me. So what is life to you Lovey that you continue to ignore the ones that truly love you and want out of this wretched hell hole of sin and evil; wickedness?

Why keep us in prison because we are in prison, and you refuse to open the gates of hell and let us; your true own out? You want, but what about our wants and needs on a whole? Why should we have to live amongst the wicked and evil to get to you?

Should we not have you already?

We are not all wicked Lovey, nor do we want and need to live amongst the wicked and evil of this world.

We are not your enemy, but yet you treat us as if we are.

As God and father, you have to do something because I told you, I do not like weakness and I've called you weak. **Evil spreads and you've done nothing constructive to stop evil in my book.** *Writing for you is beautiful, but when the one you write for is weak, it irritates me.* **You know I do not need a weak man, nor do I need a weak God. I've told you this.** *I truly love strength because strength; the power I find in spirit comforts me. You know this. I am like a happy child when it comes to strength. Yes there are days when I am weak and I annoy you, but the days that I am strong, I just want to spread my true love for you with the world.* I need better for us Lovey. I truly need better. So let December, December 2015 be ours; our better good forever ever without end Lovey. Let our good and true beginning begin and rein forever more come on now. Truly listen to Smokie Norful's song *I NEED YOU NOW* and hear me, feel what I am trying to tell you. **Life is lost without you and I know this.** I need you and our people truly need you, so truly listen and help.

If we cannot and don't listen Lovey, how are we going to hear you?

If you cannot and don't listen Lovey, how are you going to hear us?

No one should have to be tested when it comes to goodness and truth; You come on now.

Do you not test our faith?

And truth be known, IF YOU HAD WANTED LOYAL PEOPLE, YOU WOULD HAVE CREATED LOYAL CHILDREN THAT GROW UP POSITIVELY AND TRUTHFULLY TO YOU.

IF YOU HAD WANTED LOYAL AND CLEAN CHILDREN AND PEOPLE, YOU WOULD NOT HAVE INTRODUCED THEM TO WILL; GOOD AND EVIL; NOR

WOULD YOU HAVE CREATED NEGATIVE ENERGY IN THE FORM OF WILL; HUMANS.

IF YOU HAD TRULY LOVED US, YOU WOULD NOT HAVE ROBBED US OF GOOD AND TRUE LIFE; YOU. COME ON NOW. I DO NOT HIDE ANYTHING FROM YOU AND I AM NOT ABOUT TO START NOW.

YOU WANT US TO STAY CLEAN AND BE CLEAN, BUT YET YOU GIVE US AND OR LEAVE US IN UNCLEAN ENVIRONMENTS AND PLACES. NOW TELL ME, WHEN YOU DO THIS, HOW CAN ANYONE BE CLEAN; LIVE CLEAN FOR SELF AND YOU?

And don't even go their when it comes to trust and loyalty, because all I have to do is dangle my true and unconditional love of more than immeasurable truth before you.

You do not test the ones that truly love you. You do all to shield and protect them from sin and death; all that is wicked and evil come on now. Look at me when it comes to you. I want and need to protect you from all that is sinful and evil; wicked and unclean. I've told you, if I could create a new universe and earth for you that is void of all sin and evil; including unclean humans and spirits; unclean things, I would. Have I not done this sometimes in my heart for you?

So no excuses because I make none for me and I will no longer make them for you. *CLEAN ISN'T UNCLEAN, BUT YET YOU LEAVE US IN UNCLEAN STATES AND EVIRONMENTS.*

Look at what Sin and or Death said about the United States of America. When Sin talks about evil they talk about the United States of America because this land is that unclean; filthy. Hence Sin did his job and KEPT AMERICA OUT OF YOUR KINGDOM MORE THAN INDEFINITELY.

Sin and or Satan got them to MOCK YOUR EYE IN TRIANGLE. America mocks you just as my own land mocked you. Thus giving death the victory over them (The United States of America and Jamaica).

Did death not do the same thing to Ethiopia to the point of hatred on your part? Do you not hate and loathe Ethiopia? (Due to question asked by me in the spiritual realm).

DEATH GAVE YOUR PEOPLE HELL, AND THEY GOBBLED IT UP WITHOUT KNOWING THAT THERE IS A PRICE TO PAY, AND THAT PRICE IS THEIR SPIRITUAL LIFE; HELL; DEATH.

In all evil did Lovey, evil defeated you all around because evil turned billions against you. Am I laughing and glorified because of this. In truth, and in a way yes, but that is just the evil side of my mind saying **<u>I TOLD YOU SO.</u>**

You knew this would happen but yet you allowed death to devour anyway and this is sad.

But with all this said, I know death isn't victorious over you because you do have children and people that truly love you more than unconditionally. This love of truth I am more than grateful for because you deserve to be happy. I know it was not easy for you to stand aside and look as death destroyed all that you created; built.

2013 came and went and Satan did transfer his power to a human, but let that human be defeated. Death and or Satan lost because you did find true love, so truly praise you and be happy in all that you do. You are more than truly loved.

Lovey, let December be our month of righteousness and truth always.

You know December is special to me, so let this month be special to you also for the both of us. Lovey, this is my month, the month of our birth. So truly love it always like I do. Lovey, let true giving be in this month abundantly always.

Lovey, giving could be the gift of true love from me to you and from me and you to others.

Ah Lovey, truly let December be the month that our way is truly lit to you. In this month we can feel and touch you, see you always.

Ah Lovey, if only you can come back home to us in goodness and in truth in this month, the Month of December, and stay with us always and forever without end.

Lovey, this is for us, me you and our good and true people because December for us never ends.

December for us should be our each and every day of goodness and truth that never ends.

Ah Lovey, great is you and if I could give you all that is good and true; positive and clean always, I would give it to you good and true; clean and positive always without end. You are my good choice because you are a part of my good and true life; clean world.

Ah Lovey, thank you for a wonderful and great night, and yes I am hoping that before December comes, these books of ours; each one of these books are in the hands of over one hundred million plus people globally. I need to get you your house Lovey, and I need to build us and our good and true people both living and dead positively.

Lovey I need proper housing for our people.

I need to build schools and hospitals for them.

I need to plant trees that are organic and good for them.

I need you to command Mother Earth to divert her good and pure; clean waters into our land and lands infinitely and indefinitely forever ever without end more than abundantly. Our waterways can never be depleted or decrease Lovey, they must be just right and clean for us and you.

Lovey, I need to plant and plant good and true seeds with you that will always and forever grow more good seeds without end. Lovey we should not leave you, nor can we ever let evil back in under any circumstances. This is why I need impenetrable frameworks and foundations with you that can never fade or be broken down no matter what evil and the forces of evil throw at us and do. All that the wicked and evil of this world and universe throw at us bounce off indefinitely and be returned to sender. ***Lovey, evils postmark should always read; RETURN TO SENDER WHEN IT COMES TO US; OUR GOOD AND TRUE PEOPLE AND LANDS.*** No evil of any sort must reside with us. This is our clean world of truth and true happiness Lovey. Remember I complain to you time and time again about my happiness and I did tell you, you cannot make me happy. I am a complainer and a nagger, you know this. You know I will not stop nagging you, and I will get you upset; so truly listen and do something. It's over for Death and their people, so let death go. Death was never loyal to you no matter how you tried; gave us all good and true life. You cannot destroy truth Lovey come on now.

You cannot destroy good and true life and this is what Death and or Sin has tried to do. YOU WERE WRONG TO CREATE AND OR FORM MAN. HUMANS HAVE PROVEN TO YOU TIME AND TIME AGAIN THAT THEY ARE NOT LOYAL TO LIFE; GOOD AND TRUE LIFE. And don't you dare say, how dare you? I DARE TO BECAUSE I TOO HAVE SINNED RECKLESS AND RUDE.

I will not take myself out of the equation because I know my sins from conception to now. I am not flawless in my ways and or doings here on earth. So yes, you were wrong to create and or form wicked and evil people; Will. ***YOU CANNOT GIVE YOUR TRUTH AND ALL TO PEOPLE THAT DO NOT WANT OR NEED IT.***

Lovey, when you give your truth and all to the wrong people you will fall, become condemned like them. This I've learnt, hence I know; know the truth come on now.

You want cleanliness at all times. But if a person is not clean, how can you expect them to give you cleanliness; be clean?

THE HEAD CANNOT BE DIRTY AND EXPECT THE BODY TO BE CLEAN. ALL IS DIRTY LOVEY AND YOU KNOW THIS.

The head must be clean for the body to be clean come on now Allelujah. You know better, so do better not just for you but for us also.

Lovey, I need a stress free and greed free world.

I need true peace and happiness.

I need true cleanliness and harmony with all and amongst all. So no one should come into our world and say I was better off or happier where I was. I will not have this, nor will I tolerate this because I told you, I am not Mother Moses, I am Michelle and I am ignorant when it comes to certain things. You know me when it comes to the entitlement attitude and the screw face and greed. This is our new world Lovey and all negative people and attitude had better flee because I will not think twice to evicting someone's ass. So duly note this and put a clause in for the complainers. As soon as di mi nuh like dis, an mi nuh like dat start, there is the door. **_Do your part to make you happy because all is being provided for you._** Death isn't better than life, and if you want death go to death. Walk to death because in our world Lovey, death does not exist. So please whatever you do, weed out the backbiters and complainers and truly do not let any in. I refuse them. Yes I complain to you, but now that I am with you, seeing you and talking to you whilst enjoying our true and clean organic world, I will have nothing to complain about. My health is good, true love life is good; all around me is good and clean, positive and growing positively I am truly good to go.

So true and clean happiness must be all around all the time Lovey, this I need.

Wow Lovey, are we that much alike?

Are we that strict and unforgiving when it comes to certain things?

Lovey, why is life this way with us when it comes to certain things. I know good counsel we cherish beyond measure, but why is it so hard for us to listen; stay by your side?

I know the hard way in life and the hard way sucks. Tell me something, do you comprehend the hardship and hardships some of us have to face?

Do you not want to set us free and let us live again?

I know we have choices but what good is making the wrong choices all the time? I know the pain and hurt, and I truly do not want or need any more pain and hurt in my life. I do not need it for our good and true people either.

Lovey, the day is not yet done and already the devil came a calling and I had to tell her the truth. I will not stand with disobedience. Lovey I cannot condone it. My mother did it with me because she did try. I was the one to be at fault, but I have to break the chain of disobedience. I have to be like you in many instance. Yes my emotions are up and down but in this case, it is not up and down, it's straight and it must stay straight for me and you; us. Lovey, I need you.

I need a clean life and I've told you, I want no Babylonian in our family. I refuse them no matter if it's a drop. Hence my family I truly do not go around because my views are not the same as them. Listening it seems is a factor in my family. Hence I have to ask, am I like my grandmother and great grandmother in some way also?

I know we are not to mix seeds with the Babylonians, but yet billions of us do anyway. And yes I know this has nothing to do with hue; colour, it has to do with their god; the god and gods of their choosing; choice. There gods are not you and never will be you. Their god is true death, hence we are forbidden to lay and procreate with them.

Their god is the god of fire, hell.
Their god hath not life.
Their god is a liar; death.
Their god steal life and hand them and others over to hell to die. Hence your children are forbidden to marry Death's children.

Under no circumstances are we to mingle and procreate with the demon seeds of hell. Yes none of us know this, not even me once upon a time knew this, but now I know and I have to teach accordingly. Yes many will say I am spreading hate, but so be it Lovey. Like I said, **_listening to good counsel and you is a fault of us humans._** _We do not listen to good counsel because we all think we are all your children when we are not._ We have sympathy for wicked and evil people and when they massacre our asses we say they are wicked; evil and demonic. *WE FORGET THAT WE ASSIMULATED THEM INTO OUR SOCIETIES. SO WHAT WE GET, WE SHOULD NOT COMPLAIN ABOUT IT. WE WANTED THIS FOR LAND AND SELF.*

WE FORGET THAT WE WERE TO KEEP THE DEVIL'S CHILDREN AT BAY AT ALL COST BECAUSE EVIL CANNOT BE REFORMED. HENCE THE DEVIL AND OR SATAN IS KNOWN FOR HIS EVILS; WICKEDNESS AND SINS UNTIL THIS DAY.

We have not learnt our lesson, so when evil blow up our homes; places we live in, we should not complain because we as humans, we're the ones to give the devil and their children a home; a place to live. We allowed them (dirty and filthy people) access to our clean lands; environment; home.

WE ARE REAPING WHAT WE SOW. We brought bad seeds into our foundation; homes, so reap the benefits of those bad seeds and stop complaining.

WE SAY INTEGRATION WHEN YOU LOVEY SAY, SEGREGATION.

Good and evil cannot live side by side, nor can they co-exist in peace. Evil will always seek to dominate and control, wreak havoc and we see this today.

Have not evil; wicked and evil people willingly gone into another man's land; wipe out the people of that land and take what rightfully belongs to the people they kill and steal from?

Do wicked and evil people not do the same to animals?

Do wicked and evil people not start nuclear wars by destroying their own environment and the environment of others so that humans, animals and fishes alike cannot inhabit that land and or area of land? Look at Japan and Russia. So called developed nations that seek to destroy everything insight because mad and insane men want to dominate and control; dictate to others; people.

Look at the United States of America, how they invade the lands of others and massacre people in the name of so called peace. Warmongers cannot keep peace; they can only destroy; kill, and this is what America has and have done. And no, other lands like Russia are guilty of this sin. I will not talk about Babylonian lands because they were bred to kill; take humanity from their right and true path which is You Lovey. They are the devil's own hence many lands have and has brought them, into our homes to condemn and deceive us. ***Yes go ahead and say it Frank. I am a racist so and so, yes bitch to you. But guess what, I have nothing to lose because death is not on my plate and slate. I do not eat live or sleep with death, you do. <u>I know my right and rights with Life; Good God and Allelujah; Lovey, so if I am racist, I AM TRULY PROUD BECAUSE LOVEY IS RACIST TOO.</u>***

<u>As humans we do what pleases us.</u> We do not think of our community on a whole. If Lovey say Frank, do not get with this race of people, we as humans give a million and one different reasons to get with them due diversity. We want to be diverse and show the world we are not racist. So we give them (these people that do not have the same values, traditions and customs including language) a home. We deplete our resources but yet, their nations are not diverse. Could not care less about your customs, rights and traditions; values including language.

To some of you this is the godly and right thing to do because their land is riddled with violence; sin and hatred.

All this you say without knowing that <u>**THE DEVIL HAD TO GET YOU TO FIGHT FOR THEM AND WITH THEM SO THAT YOU CAN GO TO HELL AND BURN WITH THEM.**</u>

YOU GAVE UP YOUR RIGHTS AND FREEDOM; PLACE WITH LOVEY TO JOIN DEATH IN HELL. Trust me I truly do not want or need to be any of you because you're going to burn worse than a bitch in heat in hell. The demons and or daemons of hell are going to have a field day with your ass. Remember the vinegar mixed with bitter gaul unnu feed Jesus according to your book of the dead; your so called holy bible. Now think lava, fire on your part. This is what your spirit is going to get to drink in hell because there is no water there to cool your spirit, and your spirit needs water. Your spirit cannot survive without water, come on now. We all should know this. Why do you think water is so abundant in the physical and spiritual world?

Ask Lovey to bless you and see if he does not rain and or pour down water, clear water on you. So truly think because the life you save is your own.

Like I've said and will forever say. **_A man that knows not truth or have truth cannot keep the peace and or peace with anyone because true peace is not in them or with them, only death is._** You cannot say Allah, Jesus, Allelujah and kill. Many of you say Jesus is the son of God and according to your book of death, He Jesus referred himself as the *"SON OF MAN."*

SO IF JESUS IS THE SON OF MAN, HOW THE HELL CAN YOU SAY HE'S THE SON OF GOD?

IS GOD A MAN?

DO YOU EVEN KNOW GOD?

Yes I can break down God for you on your level but no, not in this book because I've told you who Lovey is in other books. And to be honest, Lovey cannot be broken down to suit anyone, not even me. Hence many of you know not about 3XY; cannot comprehend this on a spiritual, physical and mathematical level.

Back on board because I strayed. Do they (these people) accept your cultural differences and traditions?

Do they praise the same god that you do?
Are they clean and righteous?

Do they want and need the same thing as you do?

Are they respectful of your god and the holidays you choose for your god?

If conflict arises, will these people that you give a home to and accept as your own defend you, or will they side with their own to massacre and kill you?

Do they not plot and set off bombs in your country to kill your own?

You in your own land cannot speak indifferently about their profits, woops prophets and god lest they turn against you and murder you. So why give people that have not the same values as you, rights and or citizenship in your home? And yes you the religious kingdom can come at me so I can school your ass because you the religious kingdom ***WORK IN UNISON WITH DEATH. SATAN AS YOU CALL HIM, AND IT MATTERS NOT THE RELIGIOUS AFFLIATION. YOU ALL WORK FOR DEATH BECAUSE YOU ALL MAKE SACRIFICES ONTO DEATH. HENCE DEATH IS YOUR GOD.***

Life is not a god but we say he is. Lovey gave us all good and true life, but yet each and every day humans side with Death against him. As humans we take away from Life, the Breath of Life; Allelujah, but yet we say we praise and worship him; love and respect him.

Lands we are not to go into, we go into because it pleases you, and Lovey cannot tell you what to do and or say anything to you; go against your will.

We marry who we are not to marry and this suits humans just fine because you love him/her.

NOWHERE DO YOU SAY TRULY LOVE HIM/HER. YOU JUST LOVE BASED ON GREED; SILLY EMOTIONS THAT SAY PICK HIM/HER.

All when Lovey a scream at you saying Lisa, I did not pick him for you, don't marry him, yu guh ahead anyway and marry him. Now im a abuse yu, cheat pan yu, rob yu a yu dignity, yu a cry to Lovey fi a saving grace.

Now yu a halla anna sey, Lovey if only I had listened. I would not be going through this; so much pain and heartache.

Now the diseases come; riddling your body and you are saying it's not fair, what did you do to deserve this? You didn't listen that's why. Why are you getting so much abuse and pain you cry?

Am I down on you?

No.

Why you're saying?

Because I too did not listen; did not know what he Lovey was trying to tell me. All when he showed me how my life would turn out I could not comprehend. Hence you have a tat of what I went through in Behind the Scars. I cannot edit this book nor can I look upon this book. And no, there will not be a part two ever because I am so over this heartache and pain. I was spared, but hundreds of millions are not. Many are dead and gone because we truly do not listen to the counsel of Lovey, Good God and Allelujah for whom some of you call God.

<u>We cannot see the future. Lovey sees the future and know it better than me and you.</u>

I want to go home, and every time I make arrangements to go home, he closes the door to Jamaica. He tells me what will happen to me. Yes it's hard to listen because of trauma in the form of health and financial heartache and stress. Yes children and people stress also. I want to go, but I have to listen. I have to try and settle someplace else. **_He's told me where to go, but getting to the Cayman Islands is a different story._**

Wow because I too am facing the consequences of not listening. Wow, because Lovey do protect and he's shown me everyone that I call associates in my life. Hence true friends are rare and hard to find. Those that say they are your friends and or associates and or brethrens are just in your life for something. They want and do all to mess up your life; if not your life, the life of your kids; children. **_People and family, my true family, truly learn to listen to Lovey; Good God and Allelujah because he will never lead you wrong. If he says this person is a user and or taker; listen and stay away from that person. Do your best to never walk in the direction of that person no matter how lonely you get. When Lovey tells you something for your own good; it is forever ever without end. Try you best not to learn the hard way like me. Truly listen._**

NOW LOOK AT IT LOVEY, YOU SAY JAMAICA IS UNCLEAN AND WHEN SIN AND OR DEATH TALK ABOUT SIN, THEY POINT TO AND OR TALK ABOUT THE UNITED STATES OF AMERICA.

SO YOU LOVEY, GOOD GOD AND ALLELUJAH AND DEATH HAVE AND HAS POINTED OUT UNCLEAN LANDS AND PEOPLE.

BOTH ISRAEL AND JUDAH HAVE AND HAS SINNED AGAINST YOU RECKLESS AND RUDE.

BOTH ISRAEL AND JUDAH HAVE AND HAS ABANDONED LIFE. (Upward eye in the triangle, Confederate Flag for which I call the Southern Cross, and the flag of life; The Jamaican Flag.)
Judah/Yudah and Israel could not keep your own.

THEY WERE NOT TRUE TO YOU. HENCE THEY LOST THEIR PLACE

WITH YOU INFINITELY AND INDEFINITELY. ISRAEL WHORED AND JUDAH FOLLOWED SUIT. THUS BOTH LANDS GAVE UP LIFE; GOOD AND TRUE LIFE AND THAT GOOD AND TRUE LIFE IS YOU LOVEY.

The devil and his people had to make these two lands fail you. He the devil wanted control; European lands to have access to you Lovey, but you were already there. Hence interracial marriages can be found globally. Life had to go back to Eurasia Lovey we know this. *(And for some of you I am not expecting you to comprehend this).*

Black people don't weep because Eurasia (Asia as we know it) was the first not Africa and this has to do with the mountain of life. (And if I have contradicted myself from another book, please truly forgive me but this has to do with the choice that each messenger of Lovey chooses). This is hard to explain due to shifting of land and the sinking of land and lands over time.

Life has to go back to Asia despite creation. There are two race on the first level of life and or the mountain of Lovey, and those two races are the Chinese and Black Race. We are one family, hence truth must go back home. The Ying and Yang must be completed; joined as one in true peace and unison; harmony. We can no longer hate our brothers and sisters. We cannot continue to let others brand us and call us this race and that race because our foundation are the same. We are one family despite the differences humanity and or the devil drill in our heads. True love cannot hate hence this afternoon, July 20, 2015 I was being told about diversity.

What is diversity, when in the eyes of Lovey we are the same? **MEANING HIS PEOPLE ARE THE SAME; OF THE SAME FOUNDATION OF LIFE.**

Colour matters not to him because the foundation of all life is black; him and her. It's not wha. You now know the spiritual and physical, so read these books; it does tell you the difference. And no Redd, I am not promoting my books in that way. I truly do not know of a better way. Yes Jane you can go to Lovey directly, you do not need an interceder.

Yes we do you are saying Andy. Jesus is your interceder.

Now I ask you this. When you are making love to your wife, and having a good time at the bar with your friends carrying on. Do you need Jesus to intercede for you?

No, it's not like that you are saying.

Then what is it like?

Well Jesus does not intercede for me in this way. He doesn't work like that. He talks to God for me.

Well Lovey works like this. He does not need an interceder; anyone to speak to him for you. You can go directly to him just as how he comes directly to you and me.

But you talk for your people; your readers you are saying. No I do not. My readers; true loved ones and family can speak for themselves. They do not need me to speak for them. My choice for them is true, good, positive and clean life. I need them to be in an environment void of all hate, sin and evil; wickedness and death. I need them to move up and on in a positive way with Lovey; Good God and Allelujah. This is why I join with them in true peace and unison; purity of truth, so that we can live more than forevermore with Lovey; Good God and Allelujah. My goodness and or the good that I do must go towards helping them; all who need my goodness; help.

Our truth must stand forevermore, more than infinitely and indefinitely without end. So hatred you will not find in our world and or environment; kingdom with Lovey.

Colour and or hue cannot be found. Meaning no one can say well you are chocolate brown, you're pale and or white, and you're black as midnight. Colour of skin is irrelevant because the colour of my skin cannot get me into the abode of Lovey; Good God and Allelujah. He's my keep; hence evil must be kept at bay. Meaning evil can never ever infiltrate our good and true abode; home ever again.

Death had a chance but death blew it. Death has their world, so they must stay in their world with their people until death is no more. This cannot change hence you will think me to racist. And truly, I don't give a damn. Lovey is my good keep and my good world, and I refuse to let people who do not respect him come into our world and destroy him; what we have built. **<u>My god is not your god, so stay the hell out of my world and abode; kingdom with Lovey.</u>** I truly love peace and harmony you don't, so stay out of my country; world and environment. Don't want in because I truly do not want into your nasty and defiled world. Keep your condemnation and I will keep my true love all the time.

We are clean hence dirty cannot find their way in period. You are locked out forever ever without end.

Listen Andy, Lovey is on one end of the telephone receiver and you're at the other. And don't go there with the cell phone Yvette. It's the same thing.

Rob and Bob he answers your emails. You listen to the radio all the time; you'll get the right song to ease your pain. Hey it could be a message in a movie or a family or friend calling you out of the blue.

Christine Lewis did get her message in the form of a book and I did deliver the message. So Andy, I need no interceder and or anyone to speak for me when it comes to Lovey. Like I've told all of you in some of my other books, down to the underwear I wear, I want Lovey to pick for me.

Yep he can comb and doll up my nappy and happy hair too. Yes I have issues with him and I tell him this. I more than truly love him. So why should I hide things from him. I quarrel and cuss him. This is me with him and not you. I made him my true and dearest of friend. I am not expecting him Lovey to lie to me, so why should I lie to him. I will defend him but I refuse to take up arms against anyone.

WHY SHOULD I DO THIS?

WEN MI DU DIS, MI LOSE IM. SO MI FI LOSE FI MI MORE THAN BUNNUNOONUS

SEAKA UNNU? NOPE, NO CAN DO. The ass is there, kiss it.

Lovey is truly not about war and strife. He's truly about Life, good and true life that is clean and void of all sin and evil.

Some of you may say it is disrespectful to cuss Lovey and quarrel with Lovey. But I say unto you, it isn't. If you have someone that is there for you and true to you, would you not go to that person and or entity with all your happiness including troubles?

When you are mad at your spouse for something stupid he or she has done, do you not cuss her or him and quarrel with him or her reckless and rude? Some of you even hit your spouse and belittle them.

When our children are displeased with something we as parents have and has done, do they not get angry at you and voice their displeasure of you sometimes violently?

So what makes Lovey any different? I've made him my true all. The one I truly go to with all. I've also made him my beating stick because I have no true human friends. Associates I have and I can count them on one hand if I take away my children, and some family members. You cannot err you, nor can

Lovey err you for going to him with everything. My success I have to more than share with him.

My good and bad life I have to share with him.
My ups and downs I have to share with him, and in reading these books you see this. I cannot hide from Lovey nor do I want to sometimes. Family, my true family, Lovey is talked out when it comes to me. I think he's the one that need to create a universe just for himself to get away from me.

Yes my emotions fluctuates and you and Lovey knows this. Hence it's truly not easy trying to walk on his pathway when evil is all around you. We all want to get to him, but no one is willing to do the work to get there. Hence sacrifices are predominant here on earth and this is truly sad.

Truth cannot hurt but lies hurt; even kill.

We cannot say we love someone and hurt them.

You didn't truly love that person you hated them.
Know that Africa is the center and hub of life. ALL LIFE MUST FLOW THROUGH AFRICA AND IT DOES UNTIL THIS DAY. WE AS BLACK PEOPLE JUST FORGOT THE TRUE TRUTH OF LIFE THAT'S ALL. So yes, you now know that Life and Death flows through Africa. Thus Africa is the source of all.

And don't go there and say Africa is going to be destroyed. Africa cannot be destroyed because she (Mama Africa) asked for prayer and got prayer. The sins of Mama Africa will be wiped out for many lands, but for lands like Egypt, Ethiopia, Nigeria, North and South Sudan including South Africa, their sins cannot be wiped out. South Sudan I put on hold due the Lovey's school. If she does not build Lovey's School in South Sudan out of truth, and not based on religion, then South Sudan will not be saved; cannot be saved. ***I would like to say the life of Africa is dependent on this school but I cannot say this because I truly do not know. AND YOU THE BLACKS OF SOUTH AFRICA HAVE NOTHING TO WORRY ABOUT. IT'S THE WHITE SOUTH AFRICANS THAT MUST WORRY.*** A way was made for Black South Africans via Nelson Mandela but none has been made for the Whites of this land. Thus saith the Lord thy God meaning it is so. Oh Allelujah; praise your wonderful name.

27 years in prison hell.

27 years of your life taken away; robbed by wicked and evil people all because he Nelson Mandela wanted to help his own. Thus humanity knows not the significance of these 27 years. Thus for every wicked and lying White South African, add another 27 years to your sentence in hell and multiply that 54 by 48000. Now for good measure multiply that 2

592 000 by the number of days Nelson Mandela spent in prison. Death wants the years, but I want and need the days as well including the days of each leap year. Yes you can say this is truly unfair. But so is locking up someone for 27 years for your injustice and wrongs; wanting and needing to help his own.

Now it's unfair for you, but it wasn't for him. You cared not for the life and injustice of black people, but now the shoe is on the other foot and you are going to scream bloody murder.

Did you not murder this man's spirit?

Did you not take away from his good and true life?

Did you not treat blacks in South Africa unfairly and you're still doing this until this day.

So tell me, why the hell should any of Lovey's messengers cry for you and give you an all access pass to the abode of Lovey when you more than hate and loathe black people? <u>**YOU CANNOT STAND US BECAUSE WE, THE BLACK RACE ARE THE FOUNDATION OF LIFE AND NOT YOU.**</u> *So since you hate the foundation so much, get the hell out of our lands and find your decrepit own. Oh I forgot hell hath no* *home with life; nobody wants you, hence you make trouble for Life's people here on earth. Death can't stand you and the universe truly don't want you, so hell was created for you and by you. So why the hell don't all of you go there and burn forever more. Oops, I forgot, shortly that and or this is going to happen, so good and true people won't have to be amongst you and your hatred; loathsome nature and ways anymore. And that you can call racist because I was being racist.*

Yes Lovey I went there and truly forgive me. But 27 years in prison for wanting and doing the right thing. Come on man. No one should have to suffer this fate because of wicked and evil people. They invaded our space and made us slaves.

They abuse and confuse us. Give us dirty water and food to eat and drink. This isn't right. All that you've given us; they stole, and when we as a people speak up; we are persecuted and condemned for our own rights; truth. They stole you from us. They stole you and gave us their filthy gods that condemn and defile us, and for this I will never forgive them or anyone for. You are our right; you don't condemn us like this man come on now.

What right does anyone have to do this? You are our keep; protector and we defiled self with them and cause you to flee. Now look at the world, global community of humans. Bowing down and worshipping death instead of living life good, clean and true. Now tell me, how can you save us if we keep defiling self thus defiling you?

Look at me. Did you not tell me; 25 years will I be locked away in Jamaica if I go there? Did you not tell me; I will die in prison for wanting of medical care? All because of what? Cussing out the nasty and defiled cesspools of condemnation that run Jamaica; the Jamaican Government. <u>*I want and need better for my own Jamaican people, but the people and government of Jamaica do not want good for self; their own.*</u> *Hence they sold you out for dirty pieces of silver, sold Air God (Air Jamaica) and worst of all, made Germany (A German) burn your flag; our flag of life and step pan eee wid dem dutty shoes. THIS WAS THE ULTIMATE DISRESPECT.* <u>*THE TRAMPLING OF THE JAMAICAN FLAG WITH THEIR DIRTY SHOES.*</u> *You gave us; the Jamaican People your name and flag to hold up in pride, and what did Jamaicans do? Hence that ass wipe with di dreadlocks come talk bout all is okay. Eediat, bobodread, pancoot, cunumunnu, unnu lose di JAMAICAN FLAG. LIFE WAS TAKEN FROM JAMAICA AND GIVEN BACK TO GOOD GOD AND ALLELUJAH; LOVEY. SUH WEY UNNU A*

GUH DU WHEN DEATH CUM FI UNNU ON A MASSIVE SCALE?

<u>Why do you think Ethiopia lost their place with Lovey?</u> ***<u>THE SAME SHIT GERMANY DID TO THE JAMAICAN FLAG WAS THE SAME SHIT ETHIOPIANS DID IN ETHIOPIA TO LOVEY LONG AGO.</u>*** *Now some a dem an di wurl a chat bout Ethiopia has the Ark of the Covenant. A WHO DEM TINK DEM A FOOL? UNNU LOSE LIFE LANG AGO. UNNU NUH HA LIFE, UNNA HA DEATH. Life was taken from you, hence Lovey knows you not. Not one of you can or will be found in Lovey's kingdom and abode expect for the one who controls the elements. The rest of you truly good luck because unnu sell out life and live as the dead. Thus nuff a unnu a di first begotten a di dead. (Revelations)*

Unnu side with Babylon against Lovey, hence Babylon love unnu so. Unnu walk as the dead and live as the dead. Not even pretty looks can save unnu. Hence many of you have your father's genes and can be found in the land a unnu father. Thus the ether in the lots of you. ***Figure it out for unnu wey sey unnu noa, especially*** *unnu Jamaican Ethiopian batty follower that praise the dead and call death; Selassie unnu God.* Hence unnu keep the order of death because none a unnu nuh noa sey, Ethiopia were the original sells out of Lovey, Good God and Allelujah long before Adam and Eve.

They are ethers; hence they deal in fire and of smokeless fire. Yes they are the Stans of Life; Satan's own. SO TELL ME, <u>**HOW CAN ANY OF YOU SAY, UNNU PRAISE JAH AND BUN BABYLON, WHEN UNNU WORSHIP AND PRAISE A BABYLONIAN.**</u> Read unnu bible because it was told in it by profits. Yes how to rob and deceive unnu of unnu life, land, heritage, language and pride and most of all, Life Himself.

Nuff a unnu sey unnu follow Ethiopia, well so said so done. DISRESPECT IS ALL AROUND. ETHIOPIA DISRESPECTED LOVEY AND JAMAICA CAME AND DID THE SAME IN THIS DAY AND TIME. HENE UNNU A MODERN DAY JUDAS. The sellouts dem wey Satan and or Death truly love.

Hence hell is full of Black People and recruiting more literally. Unnu say unnu noa but unnu noa *nothing at all.* <u>We; no, black people cling to Africa and not all Black People came from Africa.</u>

No wonder Marcus Garvey said, **"a people without knowledge of their past history, origin and culture is like a tree without roots."** *And we the black race are trees without roots. We are scattered and we wonder like nomads; as if we have no stable place in this world; earth.*

Stop wandering and start knowing.

Stop living like the dead. You need life, so live your life good and true.

Stop letting people fool you when it comes to your roots and culture; true origins and true story, not his story. And say it when it comes to me so I can blast you. What I see and what is given to me is what I give back to you. So go ahead and say it, so I can cuss you worse than the way I cuss dem Vampires (Jamaican Government) **(Peter Tosh)** *wey suck di blood of the people an nyam di people dem flesh wuss dan drangcrow. Bunch ha demons that have and has their place in hell literally.*

Lovey, listen to RECRUITING SOLDIERS by Peter Tosh and save your true and good people. Satan transferred his power to a human in 2013 and you cannot let your people; your good and true people be defeated by him and his people. The forces of the devil is more than five billion strong globally. I am putting all my trust in you when it comes to our victory. You have true and more than true love Lovey. We must stand with you in peace and victory. Satan cannot win against you because I KNOW FOR A FACT THAT SATAN WAS DEFEATED AND HE AND HER WILL BE DEFEATED AGAIN.

It's time to come home Lovey, it's time to come home. You must lead us truthfully home to you. You cannot let us fall or be defeated come on now.

Life is truly precious with you so take us home to you in truth and not in lies and death; sin.

You know if you take a man or race from his original state of truth and feed him crap, he will live like crap and forget the truth he or she has known.

Beat him, and let him or her live in a state of poverty, he will turn from you and live like the dead; do all for death; become dead all around.

Take his manhood her womanhood and give them a false image; false hope, he/she will want to become like them that take his or her manhood womanhood over time. This is exactly what has happened to the black race. You have blacks bleaching their skin in favour of the white skin. Thus self hate and self destruction is real in the black community Lovey.

Teach a man or woman about greed, he or she will become greedy and live for greed.

So nothing surprises me when it comes to the black race. We've forgotten the foundation of life and that foundation truth; self worth.

We are the light and way of you Lovey, but billions have and has become the light and way of death. Thus billions are hell bound literally; have and has lost our way literally.

Onwards I go because I've strayed again.

Just as you (the white South Africans of South Africa) have no mercy for Lovey's true and original people, I have none for you. Yes it's an eye for an eye and a tooth for a tooth in my book on this day. There's no bleeping way I will turn the other cheek for you to damage me and my people. Well blacks anyway. And yes this is based on hue and deeds. I am making it so even though I am wrong to bring hue into this. ***And yes if the shoe was on the other foot, and it was blacks treating whites unfairly, I would hand down the exact same sentence; punishment.*** You don't rob a man or woman including child of his or her freedom and think you are going to get away with it. You will be sentenced over time and you will be cursed.

When a messenger of Lovey curses you, you are cursed for life, and in my case it is infinitely and indefinitely forever ever without end.

EVERYONE HAS A RIGHT TO LIFE; LIVE, AND NO ONE HAS THE RIGHT TO TAKE LIFE FROM THE NEXT MAN OR RACE INCLUDING CHILD.

Say it, because I do not take life from any of you. YOU ALL DO THAT ON YOUR OWN WITH YOUR SINS.

You were told, ***"THE WAGES OF SIN IS DEATH,"*** and there are no exceptions to the rules. You cannot live for death and think you are going to have life. It will never happen. All you have succeeded in doing is calling death down on yourself and death is going to take you. ***The willful and blatant killings here on earth brings humanity to hell; extinction on earth and eventual extinction*** *in the spiritual realm. So all humans have done, is succeeded in killing self.*

THE DATE FOR THE EXTINCTION OF HUMANS IS SET, AND NO ONE CAN CHANGE THIS BECAUSE IN ALL WE DO; HUMANS STILL SIN RECKLESS AND RUDE WITHOUT THINKING OF THE CONSEQUENCES.

Yes Africa houses the truth, but Africans gave up the truth to side with evil against Lovey. Now look at Africa today. Divided and fighting amongst each other for what.

Evil and wicked people keep Africa fighting so that Lovey will not return to the source; the center and hub of the universe; Life and Womb of all.

THE CENTER LEADS TO THE HEAD AND THE CENTER CAN ALSO LEAD YOU TO DEATH; DOWN.

So do your best to always go up and not down.

Why dominate and control Lovey?

Life does not dominate and control, but yet you have sick (Sikh) people that are warped and demented holding office of power. Sick (Sikh) warped and demented people that have not the best interest of their people and others at heart because they live to kill; take disadvantage of their people and others on a whole.

Just like Eve, Evening it's hard to listen. She did not listen and look at where she ended up.

I want to leave your fold and you are showing me if I leave, my life will be worse and I will burn in hell.

WE ALL KNOW DISOBEDIENCE IS A SIN PUNISHABLE BY DEATH, BUT YET WE DISOBEY ANYWAY.

We saw this with Eve; Evening but yet refuse to change our dirty ways. Lovey like I said, I know how hard it is to walk with you because stumbling blocks are in our way.

We are hindered by evil forces.

Lovey I am learning when you are good, people have a tendency to take step of you. They think they can do whatever with you and your family because you are kind. Dem libatty taking and I am fed up of this. Why hurt the people that are trying to help you? Why destroy them? Come on now.

Someone is trying to help you, don't take step of them now man come on now. Be fair. Help that person to grow so that they can continue to help you more and more if they can.

Yes this is some black people; **<u>hence I truly know what you are going through Lovey, Good God and Allelujah. YOU ARE TRYING TO HELP US AS HUMANS AND WE ARE THE ONES TO BRING YOU DOWN. DO ALL TO DESTROY AND KILL YOUR GOODNESS; YOU.</u>**

I know now that as messengers we have to walk alone to you and pray and hope that all is well with us and the lives you've trusted us with.

Yes it's not easy for you. It's hard, but this is life I guess. But why make it so hard for us Lovey?

What do you have to prove? You know the harder you make it for us is the more we want to leave. I am a perfect example of this because the beatings we get and face is brutal. Hence holding on to you is that hard and you know this. Staying with you is hard due to the different spirits of humans.

Some are wicked and evil and this is truly a shame.

Lovey I truly do not know sometimes. But like I said, the devil came a knocking; so please shut the devil down because I truly do not need her nor will I accept her as part of our good and true own and home. You know how I feel, hence I have to leave my child on his own to face the consequences of his actions. I've learned from my mistakes, hence ***I will encourage every child globally to listen to good and true counsel. If you have parents that are good and true to you, be good and true to them and listen, be obedient because tomorrow is rough. It's not easy hence the pain and pitfalls that come and they do come harsh. So truly listen to good counsel. Friends and family who tell you to be disobedient aren't your family or friends.***

Like I said time and time again in my other books; ***TRUE LOVE CANNOT HURT. TRUE LOVE PROTECTS; DO ALL TO PROTECT YOU.*** This protection I have in Lovey because as soon as I say I am leaving, he's right there to tell me the consequences of disobeying him. This is the same with our true and good earthly parents. ***When we disobey them we feel the pain later on in life.*** I did not realize this growing up, and now that I am feeling the pain with my children, I see what my gorgeous mother and gorgeous father (Lovey) is talking about. It's not easy I know, but do right for you because when the pain comes later and or tomorrow you are going to hold your belly and cry.

I've shed many tears, but I cannot go back in time to change my actions. I have to bare the pain and hopefully one day, the pain will go away never to return again. So listen, truly listen to good counsel. Lovey doesn't want us to go to hell and feel worse pain. He's securing us now because ***"THE LIFE YOU LIVE HERE ON EARTH DETERMINE WHERE YOU GO IN THE AFTERLIFE; WHEN YOU DIE; THE SPIRIT LEAVES THE FLESH."***

This is your life so truly live it. Mistakes are made because we do make them, and you are forgiven for your mistakes but disobedience, wow, some of us are not forgiven for this. We know the story of Eve (Evening), hence strive not to be like her. Strive to be the good and true you that Lovey can rely on and trust. Remember MY DAY – BOOK TWO. We are the light and way of Lovey, so respect him and you and live in accordance to his good and true laws; will.

Let no one tell you to disrespect him by breaking his law and laws. Remember you are striving to get back to him, so be one of the chosen few. Remember, many are called, but the chose are few.

Never forget this, when you are kind, good; some people will come and take advantage of you. They will overstep their boundaries with you because they take your kindness for weakness. It's July 22, 2015 and I learnt this yesterday. *You try to help others whether it be through encouragement and they lie to you; use you and abuse your friendship; goodness. Yes this is a shame but I am learning more and more. HENCE IF I HAVE NO TRUE FRIENDS IN THIS WORLD I AM TRULY OKAY. I TRULY DO NOT NEED FRIENDSHIP; THE FRIENDSHIP OF MAN BECASUE MEN ARE LIARS. HENCE I HAVE TO DO ALL TO STAY AWAY FROM HUMANS BECAUSE GOOD MORALS AND MORAL VALUES HAVE AND HAS LEFT US FOREVER MORE.*

Yes this is sad on my part to you, but it is the way it is. Many play games with other people's lives; hurt them and think it is okay when it is not. *HENCE LISTEN TO STEPHEN MARLEY'S SONG FALSE FRIENDS BECAUSE THERE ARE MANY FALSE FRIENDS AROUND; OUT THERE.* And yes I dedicate this song to myself because I thought he was true and faithful friend, but in the end I found out the liar and deceiver he was. Yes Lovey showed me him years ago and I cut the cord with him, but due to loneliness and needing someone to talk to, I started to talk to him again but how wrong I was. ***SO NOW I KNOW WHEN YOU***

CUT THE CORD WITH SOMEONE, LEAVE THAT CORD CUT. I ALSO LEARNED AND OR LEARNT THAT LOVEY DOES THE SAME THING. WHEN HE CUTS YOU LOOSE FROM HIS PROTECTIVE CORD, WORLD AND KINGDOM, IT'S AN INDEFINITE CUT. YOU CAN NEVER EVER RE-ENTER HIS WORLD AND OR KINGDOM.

And we saw this with Eve (Evening) of your so called holy book; bible. Thus billions are hell bound literally today. So please do all that you can to stay on solid ground with Lovey. Never lie to him because he does try. He tries to protect you, but we are the ones that refuse his protection. Don't make the same mistakes as me. Hence I know why people will say I am racist but it matters not to me what humanity thinks. Like I said; if I a racist, then Lovey; Good God and Allelujah is racist also.

Lovey's protection cannot be racist, it can only be true and this is what we as humans do not realize.

Lovey does not require everyone on the face of this planet to be his because we all do not belong to him like I've said. Some belong to the devil and you were told in Genesis that **_SIN AND OR SATAN HAD HIS OWN RACE OF PEOPLE HERE ON EARTH._** So know which race you are from. Life is a given, but it's not all that have good and true life.

Truly learn to listen to Lovey. If he tells you something is wrong, something is wrong. Further, don't think when you set the devil and or your so called friend and or so called family straight that the legions of hell won't come after you. Trust me they will. In anger I set this person straight in voice and words; email. Trust me this morning July 22, 2015 hell was upon me. I had a horrible sleep. Man I did not know the devil was under my bed when it comes to this person. It was if my dead grandmother a tell mi sey something and or someone aunda mi bed. And when mi rebuke dem; tell dem fi get out, two things (twin black boys) that was short hooked on to my hands. I could feel the claws that felt like staples going in my hands. Yes I squashed them; was victorious and they disappeared and I held a pillowcase in my hand in the end. Hence I've truly learnt my lesson. When Lovey say stay away; warn you about someone, truly stay away from that person indefinitely.

Michelle

It's June 27, 2015 and my personal life is getting worse and worse. I feel like I am in hell and all avenues to me are closed off.

I've been warring with God; Lovey because somewhere something is truly not right. It's like you take one step forward and all hell comes tumbling down on you. You seek stability but there is no stability there. So where do you turn.

I cannot hold on to hope when I see no hope there. I cannot battle for a race of people that cannot see their own faults; what they are doing to self.

So what about December Lovey?

Truly what about December?

I can no longer talk to you for the good of humanity because in all I see and know, I cannot find fairness in you.

I no longer have hope in you. It's faded because all I see and know is hurt and pain; not just for me but for others as well. How can you tell me to write you a book not once but twice, and nothing's been done on your part to secure our true own?

You told me you want a 25 million dollar mega mansion and you've shown me the house; home, but yet earth is truly not clean. Yes the house of your choosing is not 25 million dollars, it's way less and it's fine. But how can you come back to a dirty planet when the minds of humans are still corrupt; sinful?

My thoughts at times are not pure because I battle with you almost daily for goodness and truth; a good and clean; safe and secure place to live not just with you, but with our chosen and good few.

So what am I to do? I see myself traveling but our books are not with me except for a blue one that I gave to a female Jew. In the vision that Jew was Lenny Kravitz daughter. I had to search through my bag to find my books and it dawned on me that I did not have any, but I did find one at the last minute and gave it to her. ***So now the Jews have our blue book. Yes there was a white guy, tall and lanky, well I call him lanky was with her and he wanted a book, but I did not give him one because there was none to give him. She's the one to get the blue book and not him.*** Yes in the dream before I gave her the book, I said to her, you're Lenny Kravitz daughter and I had to chase her down; run after her to give her the book because she was in a hurry, but I am glad my efforts did not fail, the Jews; bi-racial Jews have your blue book and rightfully so. I know blue is power Lovey, hence I know your power and strength, but yet, in all I see and know, I still doubt your strength.

So yes I am taking flight again, hence my journey will never end with you even though I want it to. Not because of lack of truth when it comes to me for you, but because the pain and suffering I cannot bare anymore, and I've told you this time and time again. Lovey I am not the only one in this, and yes I am grieving because I see death, the extinction of the black race in Africa and I am powerless to save them. They are truly not my own nor are they your own. So I ask you this, <u>what was the purpose of Mama, Mother Africa asking me for prayer and telling me she's tired, if her own; African own will not listen but continue to turn against you; her.</u>

Now I ask you this yet again, what makes Mama, Mother Africa so pure when life and death started in this land and joined forces in South Sudan?

Mama, Mother Africa and her people have always turned from you, but yet you still see it befitting to try and save them, why?

Yes I know goodness still resides in Mama, but what about her people, do they truly care? How can we say life started in Africa when LIFE, AFRICAN LIFE, MAMA AFRICA'S PEOPLE GAVE UP THEIR LIVES FOR DEATH AND IS STILL DOING THIS, GIVING UP THEIR LIVES UNTIL THIS DAY FOR DEATH.

So what say you Lovey when it comes to Africa and the so called black race based on hue and hue alone?

How can they say they are Africans, but yet have not truth, the truth of life; know not the womb?

Yes the mood is different today; hence I've been battling with you all night. Yes I gave you back your book of life, put it in your hands, but you gave it back to me. So now I am tugging back and forth with you when it comes to THE BOOK OF LIFE, YOUR BOOK.

Yes I grieve today. My personal life due to my children is in ruin. I want to run away from them and it matters not if I end up in the streets, so long as I am not around my children. Honestly, I feel like you when it comes to Adam and Eve. ***I KNOW DISOBEDIENCE IS PAIN AND SUFFERING THEN DEATH,*** but yet my children are not listening. ***The children of the globe are not listening, and like my first child say, "mama it's only going to get worse."*** Lovey I know it is but what do I do, how can I save the children of this world? Lovey there is so much to talk about. So much that I see. Dreamt I was on the beach with influential people and I did not have my books with me. So there is something I am missing when it comes to our books. I keep forgetting them and this is sad. So I have to start walking with them in my bag from now on. So I was on the beach with white people and this man with a tattoo (that seemed to me like he was Mexican with the funniest blond hair which was unruly on his head) was barbequing chicken breast. He went to get one piece of chicken and it was huge, like it was ribs for which I thought was odd. This white lady was in tears, she was crying because her mate left her. Her mate was a female and she could not get over the breakup. So one of her friends that was with her offered to get her some beer to get her mind off her lost love. Lovey I can't even describe the white female bartender because the brew she poured was odd just like her the bartender. I went to a round white table opposite the crying white female and she thought I was someone else. She called me this person's name that I think was male. She told me I was the splitting image of this person. Hence I am leaving this dream right there because I cannot make heads or tails of it.

I also dreamt I was in Africa. Lovey this could be a dream in a dream hence I truly don't know.

Dreamt I was walking on sand by the sea and the water was not clean at the edges. You know how the sea water comes to shore and the water seems dirty. This is how the water seemed. This little black boy I would say around 9-12 years old came out of the water and he was pulling this long yellow cloth that I believe had some red dots in it, but not much. So I said to myself if he was not afraid of getting Malaria; a disease from the dirty water. I said to him, coming from washing and I believe he said yes and continued on his way and so did I.

I started to walk in the water Lovey which was not clean to me. There were fishes in the water and as I continued to walk these small fishes, lots and lots of them swam quickly past me. Lovey, these small fishes is like no other. It's as if their head was light but they were fishes, lots and lots of them. I know fishes mean pregnancy but so many Lovey? Are you are telling me Africa is going to give birth yet again? But the birth is not clean due to the dirty water. Lovey, I don't know because like I said, there is something truly not right in my person life and it needs to be fixed right away, but I truly do not know how to fix it because I am not being told the truth.

You know me when it comes to lies; hence truly deliver me and my children from the mess and messes they've put themselves in. I cannot take anymore because as a mother I've tried with them and I am sick and tired of them failing self and me including you. Our name is important Lovey and at the end of the day, our children bring us shame and disgrace, as well as discredit our good and true name. So how can we say our children are a blessing, when our children do bring us shame and disgrace when it comes to their friends and or the company that they keep and things that they do?

Lovey, I gave my mother trouble like I've said and I am feeling it. It's as if I am in hell and can't get out. So if I feel like this, what say them that are in hell and those who are hell bound right now?

In the dream I walked a distance and when coming back, I saw this Babylonian woman walking on the hill above me. I did not say anything to her nor did I say anything to the other Babylonian female who was carrying on old and sickly woman in her hand. **Lovey, in the dream I was upset that Babylonians were in Africa. I did not want them there; resented the fact that they were there. <u>So I will reiterate yet again, I want no Babylonian in our kingdom.</u>** They are more than forever ever locked out more than infinitely and indefinitely. *I did not see any on our mountain; hence I want none in our lands.* Their gods are their gods. You are not a part of their demonic and cruel world; hence they are to me as the Ethiopians are to you. Ethiopia gave rise to evil, hence they are mentioned in the beginning of Death's Book and you know this. I will not have any Babylonian in our land, because I refuse them. Evil seek to destroy you and make our people extinct. So why would I want them in our land and lands?

We have no claim to them Lovey, hence they have absolutely no claim to you nor, do they have any claim to our land and lands.

Things did not have to be this way, but because of hatred they made life so.

Walking on Lovey, I do not know if these were mosquitoes or locust, but a swarm of them came towards me and I think I got bit by one but I am not sure. Lovey, where did these bugs come from? So I have to wonder if the mosquito diseases that are going around is going to be brought to Africa to kill more Africans on a whole?

Lovey, so much insect and or mosquitoes?

Wow because the earth is truly not level when it comes to life and death period.

After that happened, I walked to this residential neighbourhood where African were singing along with Alaine while she sang the Jamaican National Anthem. Alaine was not there in person, it was her CD that was playing. They were singing the part that said, Jamaica land we love. Seeing this I made a fist, a black fist to show power and strength, solidarity and they did the same also. Ah Lovey, what does this mean?

The Jamaican National Anthem Lovey, is this our power and strength?

Is this, the Jamaican National Anthem our solidarity? The song of solidarity for the black race; Jamaicans and Africans alike?

Is this, the Jamaican National Anthem our unity and strength in all that we do?

Is this, the Jamaican National Anthem our power, that which will defeat all that is wicked and evil globally Lovey? Continuing to walk two black girls passed me. One was on the outside stairs as I went down and the other on the street. The second one on the street this man hit her; abused her. I told him he should not do that. And he told me to mind my own business. He didn't seem drunk Lovey, but he had a huge, bigger than normal bottle of Jamaican Overproof Rum in his hand. He came after me to fight me because of what I said. Lovey, I dragged him up and pushed him against the fence and said, "You don't know not to fuck with Jamaicans?" Lovey he swivelled up and I let him go because he was scared.

Now I think I know what this dream means. Firstly, I did interfere in African domestic affairs. Now I am being told to mind my own business, but I cannot mind my own business Lovey. Mother Africa told me she was tired and she did pay me after I prayed for her. She saw it befitting to come to me for help. She did not go to an African. **<u>She came to a Jamaican by birth and a European by descent.</u>** So I will not stop because Mama, Mother Africa is tired of the liars that infest and rape her land each and every day of her truth and riches.

She's tired of her so called Africans bringing her shame and disgrace AND SELLING HER OUT TO THE HIGHEST BIDDER.

SHE'S TIRED OF THE KILLINGS IN HER LAND.

SHE'S TIRED OF THE DISEASES.

SHE'S TIRED OF THE DROUGHT AND SAVAGERY.

SHE'S TIRED OF HER SO CALLED AFRICAN PEOPLE PERIOD.

Hence I dedicate SMILE JAMAICA by Chronixx to every African globally whether living or dead.

Listen to the part where Chronixx chronicled what Jamaica has and have given to her people, and what Jamaicans did to her. <u>You Africa have done the same to Mama Africa, hence pestilence come not just for Mother Africa, but for Jamaica as well. So truly woe be unto You the Africans and yes my Jamaican own globally.</u> Our records are there, hence pestilence will not stop in Africa and Jamaica. Yes pestilence is there for South and South Central America so truly woe be unto Spanish lands as well.

As for me Lovey, do not let me get caught up in the wars and disasters of this world. I know the depths of the sea because silent waters run deeper than we think. In all that man is trying to map and find, they will never find. They know not the truth; full truth of life and death. Hence I need to go to Guam for some strange reason but I truly don't want to. There is something that I see but you know what, I am so going to leave it alone. It does not concern me but yet it does in some strange way. Hence I know the power and strength in one punch; yes the fist of humans.

So in all that you do in December Lovey, truly remember me, and truly forgive me for all my sins and sins. Forgive my children and the good and true seeds you've given me of all our sin and sins also. Yes I know you don't want me to leave you and you are trying hard to keep me with you, but I cannot condone what is going on on earth right now. I've told you before, the true truth must be known to man; humans. They must know their end. We as humans cannot pretend and mask the truth anymore.

The clergy cannot lie to people anymore. Lives are at stake here, and I know billions of lives cannot be saved because they've accepted the mark of the beast in the form of tattoos, and some have and has signed a contract with death, hence the Free Mason Societies of the globe. The Illuminati's, Scientologists, DeLaurance and the different occults of the world including religion.

I cannot comprehend how we say we as humans love you, but hurt you in the process; continue to accept death for a place in hell.

It's beyond me why we choose death over life and disgrace and disrespect you. Yes I want and need to leave you because I see no improvement here on earth. All I see is hatred, hurt and pain, and I am caught up in this. Yes I want and need better for us, but you have to want and need better also.

I am not grounded with you when it comes to life because I don't think you truly love life, good and true life. Yes I feel like we are the left behinds in some way because true life isn't about hurt and pain, it's about truth, positive and clean energy; goodness.

Yes with sin we dirty self, but when does the war between good and evil stop?

Enough lives have and has been lost already and I've told you this. The death toll is grave and no one is taking responsibility for the lives that have and has been taken; lost. There are no winners in war Lovey, only losers because we do lose our lives and sanity, including self respect. Remember the dream I had with the people of war. I was given a play by play of these people's lives and it scared me. I'm scared when it comes to you and losing you, hence I battle with you for truth for our good and true people. Yes billions did not choose you I know this, but I did choose you. You gave me your Book of Life and I know the blue book that I gave her is not your book of life because I have it and you will not let me give it back to you. Yes we have a bond of truth, but what good is our bond of truth when I am constantly battling you; with you?

I am tired Lovey and you know this.

I am trying with my family but my family (children) is failing me. I cannot have this anymore. I need the true truth to come out because I am tired of standing in dirty water with fishes. I am tired of the swarms of bees because I do not know what this represent. Now I am seeing (dreaming) Ebola, Africans with this disease chasing me and other black people to infect them with this virus. (July 23, 2015)

Lovey what's going on?

What new strand of Ebola and or virus is out there that they are going to infect Africans with, so that this disease can travel to the Caribbean and or transmitted to other black people without them knowing?

Lovey I am tired. I am seeing death again. But this death is in the form of insects and I truly don't know what to do.

Is this the locust stage; the stage where humans are infected with manmade plagues again?

I know the devil and or death must take their own, but please truly do not let me see this in the living. Death can have his and her own, but truly let the land I am in and the lands your true people, which is our true and good people are in, be immune to these deadly and infectious diseases.

Hence I keep telling you to separate our people from the devils and or deaths people so that when death comes we are truly safe in you and with you.

I am tired of standing in dirty water with fishes passing me by. Something is not right in my life and you keep showing me fishes and I do not get it.

Where do I look because I am truly missing something?

Am I the ignorant and dark one in all of this?

Am I the scapegoat?

What are you trying to tell me?

What is wrong Lovey? Please let me know because I cannot pinpoint the wrong. I cannot put my finger on it.

Am I sinning somehow?

Am I missing something when it comes to the birth of a life?

Am I missing something when it comes to the rebirth of life here on this earth?

Lovey, under no circumstance (s) can we let life, good and true life be rebirth dirty on earth. Mama Africa cannot give birth to dirty lives again. I refuse to let this happen come on now.

Our land and lands cannot give birth to unclean and dirty lives also. This cannot happen. So come December, December 2015, let the life and lives that are born to us; within our good and true family, be clean and good, true and honest; pure and truly peaceful; harmonious and unified in truth and in you Lovey. No lies must come from the lips of these children and or life that is scheduled to be born on earth in the rebirth and or birth stage once evil and or evil's people are extinct from this earth.

Everything must be clean Lovey come on now. We cannot let unclean and dirty people come back to earth Lovey. So whatever you do, stop evil, including their dirty people and children more than infinitely and indefinitely for more than infinite and indefinite lifetimes and generations to come more than forever ever without end. Evil must never ever gain access to our lands and people ever again come on now. You know my true and good heart when it comes to you and our people. I've learnt just how nasty and cunning dirty people are; especially men. Hence I can't love you; I have to truly love you.

Lovey, I need to hold firm and true; just to my pledge with you and to you. I cannot break it, so whatever you do, continue to protect me and never ever let me or our people stray from you. Please don't make us break away from you but stay with you forevermore.

Please, let us not fail you ever again because ***I KNOW WHEN YOU WALK AWAY FROM US, IT'S FOREVER EVER. YOU DON'T HAVE ANYTHING TO DO WITH US EVER AGAIN.***

ONCE YOU DIVORCE US, IT'S FOR LIFE. WE CAN NEVER EVER COME BACK IN

YOUR FOLD AGAIN. I KNOW THIS NOW, HENCE TRULY FORGIVE ME FOR DISAPPOINTING YOU. I TRULY DID NOT MEAN TO.

PLEASE HOLD ON TO ME AND NEVER LET ME GO. I NEED YOU NOW MORE THAN EVER BECAUSE THE REIGNS OF DEATH IS FALLING DOWN ON ME. So truly bless me with your goodness. Wash me truly clean so that I can be pure again; more than clean in you and with you.

Lovey despite me quarreling with you and cussing you, truly forgive me because I want and need what is best; good and true; clean and honest; pure for us; you and me and our good and true people.

Have I sinned when it comes to the birth of life, and you are telling me I am dirtying myself?

I know life begins before conception and or before the egg and sperm is joined; united.

So now is this joining of the egg and sperm the unification of good and evil as we see in South Sudan with the Blue and White Nile?

Lovey, please because my head want to start hurting and I do not want to grasp at straws.

Lovey what am I missing?

Am I missing something to do with conception; life and how dirty it is?

No, I truly don't think so because not all life that is conceived is dirty.

Lovey what do I say to you when it comes to life and death?

I do not want to discuss abortion Lovey because I truly do not want to be wrong. I know something is locked off from me when it comes to life and when and where life starts.

I know we are born with life and death. Meaning humans are born with life and death because we were not a part of the original creation; no that's not right, we are a part of the original creation.

Lovey it's hard to explain, but at what point in our lives do we get rid of death without having to have to shed the skin; flesh? I know the beauty of life because I've seen it. The foundation of life is black I know this, but why give birth to life and death? We as the black race gave rise to life and death because all life comes thru us and no one can change this truth. But yet with knowing this, something is truly not right somewhere. There is more to know and I truly do not know what I am missing on a whole when it comes to life; good and true life.

Speaking about abortion is not for me to do because I know life is sacred to you and me. Yes I have a soft spot for this, women who have abortion. But life grows Lovey. I've written a novel that entails abortion and I've told you this, hence I shy away from the subject. My heart bleeds for mercy when it comes to this Lovey. It truly bleeds and I want and need to ask you for mercy for women who have abortion, but I do not know if it is right in thy sight. No one should have to choose the right to life Lovey but circumstances make us have to. Many are violated, raped and have to bring these children of rape into this world, and I truly do not think it is right. I know the resentment, hence I know my heart and the way I feel.

Yes I sympathize with those who choose not to bring the spawn of evil into this world. Because no man or woman have the right to violated another human being. I've lived in a community, country where the young is violated and some are killed.

I know the hurt and pain when something is taken from you.

I know it all Lovey, hence if it be thy will, in the month of December on your day, when you are forgiving sins; all sins, truly remember the women that has and have had abortions due to rape; non-consensual sex, incest and so forth. I need this for them Lovey because in truth, if the shoe was on the other foot; mine, I would do the same as them. I know my sins Lovey, and I too have thought about abortion, but did not follow through with it; hence I bare my burdens and sufferings alone. You know of my sins, hence truly remember them who have given up their unborn child, knowingly and willingly. No child should come into this world unwanted and unloved, and no woman or man should be violated and made to carry a child they truly cannot love.

No woman or man should have to look upon a child and relive their ordeal, it's not just nor is it fair. Yes tears come from my eyes for the asking Lovey, and my spirit and heart bleeds because like I said, my greatest fear is losing you. I do not want or need to ask you wrong Lovey. Hence, if my asking is truly wrong, I beg you wholeheartedly for forgiveness. I know abortion is not the final solution but for many it is Lovey and you truly cannot err them; someone that has done this.

Lovey you see the abuse of men towards women.

You see the abuse of women towards men.

You see our abuse towards children and each other globally. Now tell me in all that I see and know, how can things not affect me?

How can I not call out and cry out to you for justice and truth?

My inside is in pain Lovey, and you see and know this. I want to cry because we are so unjust to each other, and no matter how I cry out to you for justice you are truly not listening to me.

I know your hurt and pain too. You've walked away from billions of us because we lie to you each and every day.

We say we love you, but yet hurt you; cheat on you.

So what do we do Lovey?

How can we hold on to each other safely; clean and pure; honest and wise?

So as I humble myself before you, please begin to forgive me and make me whole again in you and with you and our surroundings; environment.

Michelle

It's weird how things are with you Lovey. You say you love us so, but where is the loving us so?

I cannot leave you because I am sealed to you.

At times I want to leave you but can't. Now I ask you, why the harshness in my life?

There are days when I am weak, so why leave us including me captive?

Why let us be captured?

Why are we the captured, and why can't I eliminate all facets of evil everywhere including in my life?

Lovey I am seeking a place to be on my own, but my head hurts to the price I am seeing. I truly can't afford the rent, so how am I going to live?

How am I going to face tomorrow if I can't afford today?

So where is good and true life with you?

If I cannot face life today, how are our people going to face it; face tomorrow?

I need to provide for them but you won't let me.

Now I ask you this. Why ask me for a mega mansion if you knew I could not give it to you right away?

So Lovey, how true are you in all that you do?

Why make things unattainable for us?

Why make things so hard for us if you truly did not want us to fail you in all that we do for you?

Tell me something, why let us go through all this pain?

Yes I know evil is all around, but I cannot blame all on evil, I have to blame you also; too.

Michelle

Lovey what's going on in my personal life? I keep asking you this and you are not giving me a direct answer. I know there is a lie somewhere, but I am confused. Is the lie on my side or her side?

I cannot deal with deciphering right now Lovey. I need clarity in my dream world because everything right now is clouded, and I am fed up of it. How the hell can you give wisdom and truth, when the wisdom and truth you are giving is unclear? This is bullshit on your part. No one should have to decipher the truth when it comes to you. If we do not have clarity and clear visions, will we not be confused like me?

Will we not tell lies; give lies?

Enough with the deciphering now man come on now. I am more confused than ever, and you are not helping me to find the true truth when it comes to my child. All you are doing is upsetting me by giving me dreams that I cannot decipher. I know the lies Lovey, but which side is the lie coming from? This I need to know because I cannot make sense out of the situation that this family is in. Hence I am stressed out and tired; weak from worry.

On other issues, I have to set my family straight because the mix up with my brother and his children is getting to me. I am going to blow a gasket. I do not say much and it's going to stay this way for my family, but when it comes to sister, the bullshit has to stop. My sister is there for me just like my brothers are. She has helped me just as they have helped me. When I need a twenty dollars to put food on my table she is there for me also. I cannot let my brother continue to think she is not there for me when she is, and I am sure he knows this. I refuse to exclude her because she is there for me in other areas. She has her family and I have mine, and I cannot stress her out. I am there for her if she needs me, but I will not have any member in my family think she is not there for me. Recently I've been depending on her but not regularly, once in a while for dinner when I cannot go or when my eldest cannot cook for me. So the infighting has to stop. I will not condone it. <u>**NO MATTER HOW SMALL THE FAVOUR OR GIFT IS; THAT FAVOUR OR GIFT IS STILL A BLESSING.**</u>

I AM MORE THAN GRATEFUL FOR THE LITTLE; MORE THAN LITTLE IN MY BOOK THAT MY SISTER HAS AND HAVE DONE FOR ME. I am proud of her and I am proud, more than proud of my brothers also because trust me people, they are more than there for me. Hence I have to truly remember them and do all that I can do for them. I have to save them. If I could give them, my brothers by my mother's side all that is good and true in the world, trust me, I would without hesitation, but the sibling rivalry must stop and stop now. I cannot handle anymore, nor can I handle di mix up inna mi family.

I truly do not like mix up and mix is all around, hence I have to withdraw myself from my family. My older brother's children (older brother) by my mother's side is too damn mix up, and they truly do not want me to cuss them reckless and rude. I more than loathe being caught up in mix up, hence I truly do not have friends. The he sey she sey crap is not for me. I do not need it in my family, hence I try my more than best not to know and or get involved. I stay away from my family except for my sister and brothers and my older brother and younger brother's children. So I truly don't know. My sister is my sister despite feel. We all have issues and family or not, not because I am sick, I am going to be a burden on anyone and or to anyone. I burden you Lovey enough as it is already. I have gone without and my children has and have faced hunger. Some of these things my family do not know because my children are my children an wi nuh chat sometimes. I've been down and out Lovey and you know this. You know what she did to me, hence I will never forgive her, nor will I forgive any obeah man or woman no matter the name they are called globally. My rights was deliberately taken from me.

My children faced hell and this is why I am the way I am. I forgive my children, all of them for the trouble and troubles they've given me Lovey. I do not want and need them to face anymore hell because they've faced it with me and you see and know this. Yes I do my all to protect them, but I will not stand with them in the wrongs that they do. I refuse to because they all know right from wrong literally.

Yes they don't listen but this is their decision. I cannot say Lovey, do not punish them because ***DISOBEDIENCE IS A SIN THAT IS PUNISHABLE BY PAIN AND TORMENT AND EVENTUAL DEATH IN HELL.*** We all know this, but yet billions continue on their disobedient and disrespectful ways. I cannot do this anymore because I know the truth.

Yes I told my family if my life do not pick up by September, I am going to go back home despite Jamaica being deemed unclean by you Lovey. I told you I cannot take anymore hurt and pain. I've told you I cannot take anymore because no one that is travelling on your road Lovey should have to think negative thoughts of ending their life.

You talk about truth, but nothing that you've done and in all that you've done and or you do, have you secured a good and true place for your people. We are looking to you for security and freedom from all ills and sins, and you've not prepared that good and true place for us. You keep us amongst sin. Now tell me how just and fair are you? I come to you for all, not just for me but for others and you ignore me.

Everything I come to you for, and in all you've done a part from securing me and me alone it seems when it comes to leaving you, you have not prepared truthfully for us, your good and true people. *(I know this is confusing when read but I do not have a better way to put these words).*

You tell me you want a home, but in all that you want, you do not give me the tools I need to secure you and that good and true place.

Now the sung has been sung, the Jamaica National Anthem, but where is the truth and guidance, good strength and guidance in you Lovey.

Now tell me, how can you be our guide, when you have no guidance system?

Yes I know disobedience is automatic death, but Lovey, if we have no hope, how can we become and or be hopeful?

How can you be our saviour WHEN IN TRUTH YOU TRULY CANNOT SAVE US FROM EVIL? Evil surrounds us. Evil destroy and kill us, so how can we have hope, when death controls; kill us all?

How can you be our saviour, when you leave us in unsavory situations?

Have death not taken hold of humanity and this earth?

So how can anyone believe and trust in you for all?

Lovey, DISOBEDIENCE IS A SIN THAT IS PUNISHABLE BY DEATH, YOU AND I KNOW THIS, BUT YET YOU WILLINGLY LEAVE US IN SINFUL LANDS.

Remember, Abraham of the Book of Sin and Death; man's so called Holy Bible. I am not him because I refuse to beg you for wicked and sinful people. I know not sin, I know truth, but with all my knowledge of truth, you do leave us to die in lands that are condemned to us.

You know these lands not, and instead of getting us out, you leave us here to die no matter how we plead to you. I've told you something is not right in my personal life, and instead of coming to me with the truth clearly, you've given me the truth distorted. Yes I know the curves and waves of sin, but you are Allelujah, sin cannot touch you because you are clean. So sin should not distort the truth you are giving to me or anyone.

You've shown me the power of the Jamaican National Anthem, but yet you are not true to this anthem.

Why?

Our visions are distorted.

Nothing should be distorted when it comes to you Lovey come on now. Read the Jamaican National Anthem Lovey and see for yourself.

Did we not ask you to bless our land?

I have to give you this one because you did bless Jamaica. Jamaicans are the ones to turn Jamaica into gun town; the modern day Sodom and Gomorrah. You know what; let me stop because you did keep us from evil powers. We were the ones to take up and uphold the nastiness of Babylon. We were the ones to fail you. So let me stop because you did give us great defenders, wisdom and the truth. So no, I cannot talk ill about you when it comes to this anthem. <u>**You did keep your end of the bargain. We as Jamaicans were the one to throw you away and mock you in the interim.**</u> We were the ones to lie to you, and we were the ones that could not keep true to you. So I cannot get down on you for the happenings of Jamaica and her people. <u>**We as Jamaicans say we are descendants of Africans but yet; THE TRUE AFRICA WE COULD NOT KEEP, AND THAT TRUE AFRICA IS YOU.**</u>

JAMAICAN NATIONAL ANTHEM

Eternal Father bless our land
Guard us with Thy mighty hand
Keep us free from evil powers
Be our light through countless hours
To our leaders, Great Defender,
Grant true wisdom from above
Justice, truth be ours forever
Jamaica, land we love
Jamaica, Jamaica, Jamaica, land we love.
Teach us true respect for all
Stir response to duty's call
Strengthen us the weak to cherish
Give us vision lest we perish
Knowledge send us, Heavenly Father,

Grant true wisdom from above
Justice, truth be ours forever
Jamaica, land we love
Jamaica, Jamaica, Jamaica, land we love.

So with all this said Lovey, strengthen me and the community and environment you've given me and our good and true people globally. Let us uphold the Jamaican National Anthem in truth because you are our good and true defender; protector.

Let us be true to you always. Hence I ask you to take lies from our lips, genes and thoughts more than infinitely and indefinitely forevermore. We cannot lie to you Lovey because in truth, you do not lie to us no matter the distortion of my dreams. I am the one that cannot decipher and comprehend them as of late. Hence I have to get back to my higher learning with you. You did give me life to keep and I aim on keeping it (life) because you do trust me in the living and spiritual realm. So as I secure you in goodness and in truth, secure me also in goodness and in truth so that I can secure our good and true people in goodness and in truth. Like I've told you, my greatest fear is losing you, so please whatever you do, do not make me lose you because when you are gone, you are gone forever. I cannot get you back and this is what has and have happened to my many nations in this day and time. **The black race not based on hue must clean** *themself up so that they too can be saved. Shortly death is going to take on a massive scale and there is absolutely nothing humans can do about this. This death has been commissioned, and this death must be fulfilled. Thus saith the Lord thy God meaning it is so.*

So Lovey I have to put and or set my family straight because along the way, we are not grateful for the help no matter how small the help is.

I am, hence I remember gratitude. And despite me getting down on you Lovey, I am truly grateful to you because you are there with me in my storms. I complain a lot because I am expecting so much more from you. What I do for you; us, I was not expecting to go through so much pain and hardship and you know this. And yes this is why I need to prepare a stress free and rich environment for me, you, our good and true people, the environment itself, the good and true waterways; earth itself and yes the universe including our spiritual realm.

Yes I know it is written that disobedience is a sin and is punishable by death. I will not change this **BECAUSE WHEN WE SIN WE GO AGAINST YOU LITERALLY.**

Michelle

Wow do I feel so obsolete
Withered and old

Why do I have to be this outdated
This unfriendly

Damn, I am like Turbo Pascal and COBOL.

Put in the junk pile and filed under ancient.

It's Friday and I have absolutely nothing to do.

No friend to call up and say hey, let's go see a movie.

Damn loneliness stinks.

How am I coping?
Will I start talking to myself?

Ancient am I
Ancient
Soon to be extinct like them dinosaurs.

Michelle
June 19, 2015

I am not driven
Man why can't I be like the wind?
Why couldn't I take myself away to some other land; world?

It sucks being one; alone.
It sucks walking alone.
It sucks to be me.

Michelle
June 19, 2015

The tears come
I am alone

Sad am I
Yes I feel a pang of jealousy
Wish it was me moving to a house in a different neighbourhood.

But yet with this, I feel like an outcast; detached from it all.

I am but a dinosaur in a maze made to keep me trapped; caged.

Michelle
June 19, 2015

I feel so tired and weary today.
I need to end this book and start on part two.

There are many writings I did not include in this book that I will include in part two.

There is still more that I want to include, but my dream world has become confusing on a more personal level.

There is something I am missing in my life that I cannot figure out and hopeful the truth, true truth will come out one day. Too much confusion; something doesn't add up. So confused am I, really confused; paranoid.

Lovey you see and know my trials and tribulations hence I've told you, I have no issues in walking away from my family more than indefinitely. My world and truth is not their world and truth, hence I've made you my all and true family including beating stick. I come to you with everything and it's going to stay this way.

I need rest now. I have to come home you. I have to settle down with self and spirit when it comes to you and the goodness you have for our good and true people.

Lovey as for my last child. I leave him and his dilemma in your capable hands because like I said, there is a lie somewhere, and the truth needs to be told. I cannot continue to be stressed out over something that I cannot see clearly, nor do not add up.

I need the full truth to come out because you know how I feel about Babylonians; not due to hue but due to lies.

One lie has been told already and I will not tolerate it; hence I told you specifically, I do not want or need any Babylonians in our kingdom. Separate us because I make no provision with you for them. I truly do not care if there is a mixture of race, I do not want any in our family. Their god is not you and I refuse to bring some other god and or gods into our clean and true environment. You are all I need, and it's going to stay this way. I refuse to cheat on you and make myself dirty, so truly, **_NO OTHER GOD OR GODS ALLOWED MORE THAN INFINITELY AND INDEFINITELY WITHOUT END._** I am more than serious and true when it comes to this and you. No one should come and take you from us ever again. I refuse this (cheating and dirty lifestyle) and you had better too lest I divorce you for lack of truth; cleanliness. And yes you can call me racist for this, but I remember the lie Lovey. I remember the lie and I will not have it, nor will I have anyone telling lies on you.

I KNOW THE COST OF LIES AND THE COST IS DEATH. I WILL NOT DIE FOR A BABYLONIAN NO MATTER IF THEY ARE IN MY FAMILY OR OUTSIDE OF IT. I DON'T WANT THEM NEAR. NOR DO I WANT THEM NEAR YOU AND IN OUR GOOD AND TRUE KINGDOM; ENVIRONMENT. THEY CAN KEEP THEIR GOD AND GODS OF DEATH. I HAVE LIFE; YOU, AND I AM MORE THAN TRULY AND UNCONDITIONALLY KEEPING YOU.

Their god and gods are not you; hence I want none in our fold. I will not have anyone take you from me or our people again. ***True life is our right and that right is you.***

I don't care if the whole world deem me as a racist. If the shoe was on the other foot, and knowing what I know given what I've seen in visions, literature read, and as taught by you, they would do the same thing. I will not provide a home for evil. ***MY ANCESTORS OF OLD DID THAT AND LOOK AT***

THE COST TO THE BLACK RACE – HUMANITY UNTIL THIS DAY.

Our life and rights have been taken from us. This is why I ask you Lovey for more than impenetrable frameworks and foundations so that evil and sin, all facets of sin and evil cannot reach us or conquer us ever again. They cannot dominate and control us anymore. Nor can they take you away from us anymore. With these books Lovey, humanity is on their way of finding you, so truly let them find you.

Those cannot find you; meaning those that have their name and number written in deaths book forevermore must know their end. They have the number, so many can calculate the time they will spend in hell. The value of one good is 10 000, but the weight of one sin is 48000 years burning in hell.

You gave me life; good and true life Lovey, so why should I take that good and true life from you?

Why should I continue to give wicked and evil people a home?

Evil tries to destroy you, so why shouldn't I protect you; do all to protect you here on earth and in the spiritual realm including the universe?

I've told you, true love is rare and it is also true.

TRUTH AND TRUE LOVE CANNOT PROTECT THE WICKED, IT CAN ONLY PROTECT GOOD, GOOD AND TRUE PEOPLE INCLUDING CHILDREN, THIS EARTH AND UNIVERSE INCLUDING GOOD AND TRUE SPIRITS THAT ARE IN THE SPIRITUAL REALM.

I cannot say I truly love you and go against you.

I've told you I want to leave you, but it's not because I don't truly love you or I want and need to be disobedient. I cannot take any more pain, and this is why I want and need to leave you.

You are not hearing me, and **_listening does not go one way, it goes both ways._** There is only so much suffering that I can take when it comes to you. Besides I want to be able to feed people and provide for them that are in need. I need to provide positively and good for good and true people that are calling out to you for help come on now.

Why should our people be down and out?

I've told you disobedience is a sin that is punishable by death, so why leave our people in disobedient and condemned lands?

Why you do this Lovey?

Are you not being disobedient as well?

You cannot want us to listen to you and you are not listening to us?

You do not conquer and control I know this.

You do not lead falsely even though I accuse you of this. So why not do right by us, me and you and our good and true people starting this December, December 2015?

Let our goodness and truth grow all year round.

As of this December, December 2015 and even before, let these books find the right people and save them. All who need saving; (except for Germans, Nigerians, wicked and evil Jamaicans, Ethiopians, Babylonians, people from Luxemburg because you have a bone to pick with these people, and until now you can't tell me why, White South Africans and Americans to name a few). Let these books save them and let these books provide good, clean and positive homes and food including finances for those that truly need help. All good and true people should find pleasure, true pleasure and peace that is positive and true from these books. And Lovey, truly no Babylonians are allowed because in truth, my spirit on earth and in the dream world including spiritual realm truly resent them. I will not provide for them nor will I provide for a German or Nigerian.

You know I will never ever without end provide for an Ethiopian, so you have absolutely no worries there. I've said my peace hence truly help me to finish part two of this book soon.

Michelle and Michelle Jean

There is so many things that I am realizing Lovey and I have to ask, how do you cope?

How do you stay sound and grounded in all of this?

How do you deal with humanity and the different gods and personalities that are out there?

I have ask; how do you stay sane and true to self?

I see firsthand what happens to us when we don't listen to you. I know that when we don't listen to you, all hell is opened up to you and you do feel pain; hurt and sorrow.

You do get used and abused brutal.
You are stressed.

Lovey, I know my wrongs, but so much abuse though?

Am I wrong in choosing you?

Am I wrong to want and need good life; a life void of all hurt and pain; stress and lies?

What do you need for self; yourself Lovey?
What do you need for me and you?

What do you need for our good and true people?

What do you need for this earth and universe?

In all I see Lovey, I see the beauty of life, but in all the beauty I see, can a person; a man or woman stay lonely?

Do we not need good and true friendship in the flesh as well?

Yes I know you are my bestest friend, but what about human friendship? Do we not need this also?

I know the world I grow up in Lovey; hence abuse is prevalent. Men beating the good woman he has while keeping his mistress satisfied.

She works hard for him and he takes her money; the money she's worked hard for and support another woman. HENCE I WOULD ADVISE EVERYONE TO WATCH GLORY TO GLORIANA.

THIS STORY IS A TESTAMENT TO A LOT OF US BLACK WOMEN THAT WANT AND NEED BETTER FOR SELF, BUT BECAUSE OF WICKED AND EVIL MEN; THEY BREAK US DOWN AND KEEP US TRAMPLED DOWN.

I know the struggles Lovey because I too have faced them. So yes, I know your struggles and pain also because in truth, we as humans do the same thing to you each and every day. We keep you trampled down and we keep you in pain; cause you to cry because of the sin and sins that we as humans do each and every day.

As humans we truly do not think of you because if we did, so much crime and violence would not be on earth; this land that we call home.

We as humans would be our brother's keeper in a good and true way.

We would not create nuclear weapons, guns and ammunition; diseases to destroy and kill each other.

If we truly cared about you Lovey, we would not disrespect you and go against you.

I KNOW LOVE IS OF THE DEVIL. WICKED AND EVIL PEOPLE LOVE; SAY THEY LOVE YOU BECAUSE TRUE LOVE AND RESPECT IS NOT IN THEM. SO THEY LOVE TO FOOL YOU, KEEP YOU SATISFIED WHILST HURTING YOU IN THE PROCESS.

I know true love; hence I talk to you and tell you about this, true love. We need the truth Lovey. We need your true love at all times.

I know you are gone from billions, but I care not for the billions you've lost because these people were not your true own. I, however care about our good and true people that will uphold your good and true values and be strong in you. Our good and true people that will find strength and power in the Jamaican National Anthem and uphold the values and truth of this anthem, and more importantly You.

I know you; hence I truly do not want or need to lose you. You are our gain Lovey. So why should we lose our asset and assets when our asset and assets is you. Look at my life and the life of our people Lovey. I know shame and disgrace is coming to my family and I pray this morning that you take this shame and disgrace out of my way; my family's way in a good and true way. I truly do not need any more heartache and pain Lovey; hence I am coming to you with all. Truly help me to fix the mess and messes; problems in my children's life and in my life. Right now we need you more than ever.

I cannot let the devil devour us; hence I am truly sorry for the heartache and pain I've caused you.

Michelle

OTHER BOOKS BY MICHELLE JEAN

Blackman Redemption – The Fall of Michelle Jean
Blackman Redemption – After the Fall Apology
Blackman Redemption – World Cry – Christine Lewis
Blackman Redemption
Blackman Redemption – The Rise and Fall of Jamaica
Blackman Redemption – The War of Israel
Blackman Redemption – The Way I Speak to God
Blackman Redemption – A Little Talk With Man
Blackman Redemption – The Den of Thieves
Blackman Redemption – The Death of Jamaica
Blackman Redemption – Happy Mother's Day
Blackman Redemption – The Death of Faith
Blackman Redemption – The War of Religion
Blackman Redemption – The Death of Russia
Blackman Redemption – The Truth
Blackman Redemption – Spiritual War
Blackman Redemption – The Youths
Blackman Redemption – Black Man Where Is Your God?

The New Book of Life
The New Book of Life – A Cry For The Children
The New Book of Life – Judgement
The New Book of Life – Love Bound
The New Book of Life – Me
The New Book of Life – Life

Just One of Those Days
Book Two – Just One of Those Days
Just One of Those Days – Book Three The Way I Feel
Just One of Those Days – Book Four

The Days I Am Weak
Crazy Thoughts – My Book of Sin
Broken
Ode to Mr. Dean Fraser

A Little Little Talk
A Little Little Talk – Book Two

Prayers
My Collective
A Little Talk/A Time For Fun and Play
Simple Poems
Behind The Scars
Songs of Praise And Love

Love Bound
Love Bound – Book Two

Dedication Unto My Kids
More Talk
Saving America From A Woman's Perspective
My Collective the Other Side of Me
My Collective the Dark Side of Me
A Blessed Day
Lose To Win
My Doubtful Days – Book One

My Little Talk With God
My Little Talk With God – Book Two

A Different Mood and World – Thinking

My Nagging Day

My Nagging Day – Book Two
Friday September 13, 2013
My True Love
It Would Be You
My Day

A Little Advice – Talk
1313, 2032, 2132 – The End of Man
Tata

MICHELLE'S BOOK BLOG – BOOKS 1 – 20

My Problem Day
A Better Way
Stay – Adultery and the Weight of Sin – Cleanliness
Message

Let's Talk
Lonely Days – Foundation
A Little Talk With Jamaica – As Long As I Live
Instructions For Death
My Lonely Thoughts
My Lonely Thoughts – Book Two
My Morning Talks – Prayers With God
What A Mess
My Little Book
A Little Word With You
My First Trip of 2015
Black Mother – Mama Africa
Islamic Thought
My California Trip January 2015
My True Devotion by Michelle – Michelle Jean
My Many Questions To God

My Talk
My Talk Book Two
My Talk Book Three – The Rise of Michelle Jean
My Talk Book Four
My Talk Book Five
My Talk Book Six
My Talk Book Seven
My Talk Book Eight – My Depression
My Talk Book Nine – Death
My Talk Book Ten – Wow
My Day – Book Two